# Country Seasons

*Also by Phil Drabble*

BADGERS AT MY WINDOW
MY BELOVED WILDERNESS
DESIGN FOR A WILDERNESS
PHIL DRABBLE'S COUNTRY SCENE
OF PEDIGREE UNKNOWN

Phil Drabble with Tick and a ferret

# Phil Drabble
# Country Seasons

photographs by
### Stanley Porter

## BOOK CLUB ASSOCIATES

LONDON

This edition published 1977 by Book Club Associates
by arrangement with Michael Joseph Limited

© 1976 by Phil Drabble

Printed in Great Britain by
Hollen Street Press Ltd at Slough
and bound by Dorstel Press at Harlow

# Contents

## Spring

## Summer

# Autumn

# Winter

The illustration appearing on page 71 is reproduced by the kind permission of the Peak Park Joint Planning Board.

# *Foreword*

## by Johnny Morris

Those who talk affectionately of the dear dead days are frequently criticised by our progressive thinkers for being sentimental: to regard times past with a wistful nostalgia is simply being unrealistic and a refusal to face facts. And yet it occurs to me, as it must to many, that our nostalgia could be an instinctive knowledge that we have left our intelligent and practical way of life far, far behind and there is no possible way that we can turn back, say we are sorry and try again. With the passing of the horse, it seems, we have lost our horse sense for we are half suffocated by a world of theory which is propounded by people who try to manipulate life into what they think it ought to be instead of accepting life as a physical and spiritual condition. For a society to make laws about discrimination is enough to send the Gods rolling about with laughter. Our plans for living are discussed by committees and put down on paper. We live in a paper world populated by paper people. And the harder they try to put things right the more it seems they make things go wrong. We need a real whiff of the true facts of life and just to start with I would suggest a read about Phil Drabble's sanctuary in Staffordshire. It's quite an experience.

I remember I first walked this beautiful haven with Phil many years ago but I was well aware after we had been wandering and chatting for a few minutes that he knew what every blessed bird and mammal was up to. It's one thing to identify a creature, to wonder at its beauty and thrill at its movement, but it is surely a most patient and observing mind that can add to all that, discover the motives of the frogs, the stoats, the Bagot goats, the badgers, the foxes, the herons, the roe deer and the ducks. They live all around him. He understands and provides the environment they need, and being intelligent creatures they know when they are on to a good thing and stay put. Which of course was Phil's main motive: to hold this very varied collection of wildlife together naturally.

In *Country Seasons* Phil tells us how he manages to do this. What a blessing that he is able to write so entertainingly and well, for he writes as he speaks and I've listened to him with fascination many, many times. I remember he once said to me after we had both appeared on the television programme, Animal Magic, "You know I always pick up a wrinkle or two from Animal Magic." "Pick up a wrinkle or two" was how he put it. *Country Seasons* is crammed with wrinkles for Phil is a most crafty wrinkle-picker. Well would you train your dog with chocolate drops and Indian corn? Chocolate drops, yes. Indian corn? Well, read on and you'll find out, and you will also surely find out that Phil Drabble is a most happy man. He does what he wants to do, lives in the intelligent environment of the animals.

*Johnny Morris*

# Acknowledgement

Parts of this book are based on material which originally appeared in my weekly column in the *Birmingham Evening Mail* and my thanks are due to David Hopkinson, the Editor, for his encouragement to produce them in book form.

P.D.

# Spring

# 1. Halfway house for the helpless

Ever since I was a schoolboy, I have spent a great deal of my time in rearing and keeping British animals and birds. Young creatures often end up at our house because they have been acquired as pets by people who didn't realise the difficulties of keeping them or just what a tie they would be. When the novelty wears off, they give them their liberty, which means throwing them out into a world with which they are totally unfitted to cope.

A few land up in zoos and some are passed on to naturalists like me. I never mind because I have learned so much from creatures in the halfway house between captivity and wild freedom.

Our roe deer and badgers live in an enclosure by the house which includes meadow, pool, bracken, rushes, marsh and woodland. It is the

Bottle-feeding orphan leverets

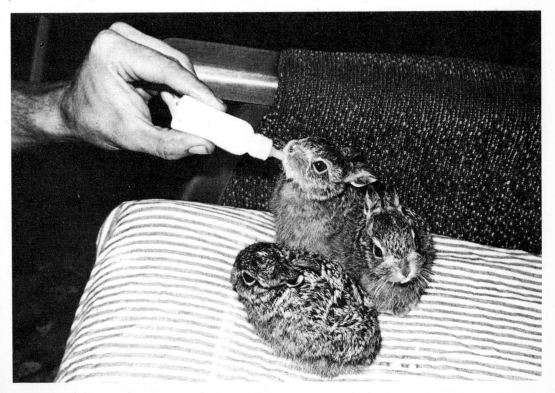

exact type of country they would choose for themselves if they were wild. By watching them at all hours from the window, I have been able to learn more about their habits than if I had spent the same time in wilder places more difficult to observe.

It is not practicable to give the roe deer complete freedom because there are no wild roe in the Midlands, and the Forestry Commission would not take kindly to the introduction of a species which could damage their young trees. The badgers were once completely free to come and go as they liked, but I have had to enclose them now because one of them was hanged in a snare. She wasn't on our land so I had to shut the survivors in the enclosure for their own safety.

At various times I have kept foxes, stoats, weasels, owls, hawks, a Bewick swan, and a wide variety of songbirds; and it was possible to give nearly all of them complete liberty when they could fend for themselves. I even had two albino rooks and a common rat called Haw Haw, which was delightfully tame and a far nicer character than his namesake.

The one British animal that I have never made a success of rearing is the common brown hare, which for some reason seems particularly difficult to rear. The first time I tried was with a litter of leverets which arrived one Saturday morning just as we were setting off to stay the weekend at a country pub for a broadcast. Their mother had been killed by a machine mowing hay, leaving four orphaned leverets no bigger than golf balls.

My wife packed a hot water bottle, and we bought a tin of baby food and a doll's bottle at the first town we passed through. And since I feel only half-dressed without my dog, we also had my old whippet-lurcher Dinah with us. It turned out to be one of the few pubs we have stayed at which has objected to dogs, but it was not difficult to persuade the landlord that Dinah was far more civilised than me. We did wonder what he would have said if he had known that there were four leverets in his dressing table drawer.

My wife filled the bottle from the hot tap every few hours, and we took it in turns to get up in the night to give them baby food through the teat of the doll's bottle. It was all to no avail and it might have been better if the mowing machine had killed the young hares as well as their mother. One by one, they weakened and faded till, by Monday morning, they had all died.

I have tried to rescue litters of leverets several times since without success. The few people I know who have got them started have usually lost them with disease within a very short time.

The one person I know who had consistent success was my old friend, Miss Frances Pitt, who farmed a most pleasant estate near Bridgnorth. She was a distinguished naturalist, and I believe that what she couldn't rear must have been unrearable. She certainly seemed to find no great difficulty with hares, and when they grew up she let them loose in her garden which was surrounded by a fox-proof fence. There was usually a semi-tame hare or two pruning what remained of the roses outside her drawing-room window. She simply said that it was difficult to be a good gardener and a naturalist. It was a philosophy she took so far that I once saw two leverets grazing off the pile on her study carpet.

A few weeks ago a farmer rang me to say that his sheepdog had killed a hare which was obviously a nursing mother, and how could he cope with her litter of leverets? I didn't hold out much hope but told him what I knew and was surprised when he rang later to tell me of his success. He had had to force feed them to begin with, but they took freely to the doll's bottle and then supplemented their milk by grazing clover on his lawn. They came into the farmhouse where, far from being proverbially timorous, they were monarchs of all they surveyed.

Knowing the difficulties, it is tempting to write-off such success as beginner's luck. I prefer to believe it is the stockman's equivalent of gardeners' green fingers. It is a wonderful gift to have for it must not only have given him the joy of achievement, but has given his leverets a chance of freedom against which I for one would have laid heavy odds.

# 2. Instant mums

One of the pleasant things about living in the country is that it is possible to feed to a great extent on the produce we grow for ourselves. I do not mean that my hands are horny from wearing out the handle of our spade, or that my back aches from digging the garden. I have never been fond of the punishment hard labour metes out for the sake of a few spuds or a cabbage or two.

My pleasure comes more from keeping enough stock about the place to make us more or less self-sufficient for meat and eggs. We let our hens run free on fresh grass and scratch for insects among the leafy litter of the woodland floor. In return, they lay great brown eggs with golden yolks far richer than the pallid jelly pumped out by birds serving a life

Tick 'herding' the silky and her foster children

sentence in battery cages. We let about a dozen cockerels grow till they weigh ten to twelve pounds each. They fill the oven like turkeys and come to the table as mountains of succulent flesh.

We reared three geese and some guinea fowls the year before last. So this time I thought home-grown ducklings would make a pleasant change. I have kept a flock of silky bantams for the last twenty years or so, although they are a gastronomic flop. Their skin is almost black, giving the flesh a hue of deathly grey. They would be unappetising to all but the colour blind. When they have laid about a dozen eggs, they go broody. I am normally far too practical to suffer gladly those who work to rule but my silkies have other attractions. They are so pretty, tame and gentle that they make the most delightful pets and it would take a harder heart than mine to serve them up at table.

Even their propensity to broodiness can be an advantage. Their instinct for motherhood is compulsive. When they have been sitting on eggs for a few days, they not only cease to care about the colour of their offspring, they don't even mind what species they are. I have given them the eggs of black hens and white, large eggs and small, pheasant, partridge and guinea fowl eggs with equal success. They sit on them all with devotion until they hatch. Then they rear them as if they were their own flesh and blood.

This year I didn't even let them hatch the eggs. I bought twelve day-old Aylesbury ducklings and put six under each of two silky broodies. I was careful to do this at night, so that the hens could not see the shape and colour of the foundlings I had foistered on to them. All they could sense in the darkness was that the hard unyielding eggs they had been sitting on had suddenly been transformed into a downy mass of cheeping innocence.

As soon as the ducklings felt the warmth of the silky feathers their cheeps of protest quietened to content. By the time dawn broke, the hens were happy to have become instant mums. They had exchanged crooning endearments all night. So far as they were concerned, the ducklings were hatched from their eggs and were their chicks. The fact is that they were hatched in an incubator so that they had never heard the quack of a female duck. They simply associated warmth and protection with the affectionate voice of their silky foster mothers.

For a couple of days I kept them in small runs on short grass, with bowls of food and shallow dishes of water. Then as soon as they were strong enough, I let them run about. The hens could take them where they liked in the paddock near the house. I changed their water dishes for a slate trough which had started life in a cottage cellar as a bacon salter. It is easily cleaned and shallow but holds a surprising amount of water so that the ducklings love it. They spend their day commuting between the water and the shed. There they sleep and eat, resting for long periods with one of the hens on the grass between the two. Then they spread out in line, quartering the paddock for flies which they are astonishingly adept at catching in their broad bills.

Tick, the pointer, is enchanted with them. She doesn't take much notice of the domestic chickens, but the ducklings must have some subtle scent she associates with game. The first time the hens brought them out, I noticed Tick's sensitive nose testing the breeze. Then she stalked off with the stealthy gait she uses for pheasants. She dropped her head till it stuck out straight in line with her back and moved slowly towards them.

Normally when she isn't quite certain where her quarry is, she stops, listens and watches, to add the clues of sight and hearing to the delicate evidence of her nose. Then at last, when she gets within arm's reach, she crouches down and allows me to creep up too so I may share the delights she has discovered.

But these ducklings were not hidden like pheasants in deep bracken or prickly brambles. They were on short turf, beside their slate water trough, plain for all to see. Yet Tick seemed as if she couldn't believe that I had any idea that they were there. She went through all the motions of stalking them till she was close. Then she crouched down, glancing at me with the whites of her eyes showing, to make certain I had not missed the prize that she had revealed.

The little birds' gamey perfume was obviously intoxicating. She wallowed in its luxury, enjoying the sight and sound and smell, without daring to move a muscle lest she break the spell. The temptation to touch as well as look was almost overwhelming but she resisted it. It was a delightful example of how selective breeding and careful training can channel the hunting instincts of a very intelligent dog.

# 3. The empty landscape

You can argue about hedges till you're blue in the face. If you're a farmer, you will probably want them out; hedges occupy land but contribute nothing to the kitty when the harvest comes around. Some say they harbour both rabbits and insect pests. And nobody doubts that they get in the way of the juggernaut machines that have so largely replaced horses and the men who drove them.

If you are not a farmer, the odds are that you hold the opposite view. The patchwork quilt would not be England without hedges to etch in

A mutilated hedge, an all too-common sight

the pattern. When they are grubbed out, the pitiless wind whistles unhampered over vast prairies of plough and, at best, dries the topsoil into a brittle crust through which tender shoots cannot force their way. At worst, the hard crust will crumble and be blown away in dust storms.

Both views are right. It is perfectly true that farmers have sunk their cash into expensive machines that have cut the labour force from a man to about every forty acres to a man to two hundred or more. Although they are still low by modern standards, farm labourers' wages have multiplied more than ten times in my lifetime. They priced themselves out of their jobs and were forced to drift away from the land to factory life. Fewer people on bigger machines need ever bigger fields to cultivate, and whether we like it or not, the trend seems bound to continue.

Another farmer's answer to complaints about disappearing hedges is that hedges were no more than a passing fashion. He will tell you that most of them only appeared within the last century or so – because they were planted at the time of the Enclosure Acts. Before that, England was mostly farmed on the open field system and nobody raved about patchwork quilt views in those days. Hedges were cultivated to keep stock in because of the changing methods of farming. Now that mechanisation is changing methods again, hedges are as obsolete as a horse-drawn plough.

Naturalists deplore the disappearance of hedges for reasons quite unconnected with aesthetic views or farming economics. Countryside with hedges supports thirty to forty different species of birds. The same land will have no more than five or six species if you grub out the hedges. There will be no nesting cover except for birds like skylarks and partridges which nest on the ground, and no safe roosting either. Blackbirds, wrens, tits, finches and warblers will retreat to the edges or disappear altogether.

I know plenty of farmers who would reply that they farm to grow food, not listen to the dickie-birds; so why the fuss? Here they are on weaker ground. However sophisticated their modern pesticides, insects seem to have a wonderful capacity for developing resistance to them. But no pest has yet managed to produce an effective defence against its natural predators. The argument that birds were here before hedges were planted in quantity and will therefore be here when hedges go again, does not hold water either.

A couple of centuries ago, the countryside was far more densely and universally wooded than it is now, and most of our wildlife, including deer, badgers, foxes, insects and birds, are really woodland species. It so happened that the Enclosure Acts coincided with the heaviest clearance of woodland, and many dispossessed creatures were only able to adapt themselves to living in more open countryside because it was criss-crossed by a network of hedges that took the place of woodland.

These hedges were not only useful for concealment and nesting cover, they were vital as the routes by which animals and birds – and even plants – moved from place to place. Animals ran along their base and tunnelled in their banks. Birds flitted from bush to bush, dropping the seeds of plants as they did so. The result was that if some catastrophe wiped out a local population by disease or enemies, it was soon replaced by others of its kind finding untenanted territory as they travelled the hedgerows.

It is often possible to establish the age of a hedge by taking a thirty-yard stretch and counting the species of plant and tree it contains. If there are only two species, it is unlikely to be older than the Enclosure Act of 1800. It will be about a hundred years old for each species you find. So if there are ten species of different bushes and trees, it was quite likely planted by the Saxons who put hedges along their boundaries a thousand years ago. They were probably the original rolling English drunkards who made the rolling English roads, and their hedges lurch along with no control over where they go to next.

The Crown Estate Commissioners administer over 230,000 acres of Crown lands. They started a scheme to give grants to tenants for each tree they preserved when they trimmed their hedges. When they do give a tenant permission to grub a hedge out to make way for his giant machines, they insist that he plants twice as many trees as he takes out somewhere else on his farm as provision for the future. Other landlords, please follow suit.

# 4. *The thrush in my study*

A surprising number of people ring me up to ask how they should rear some young bird or animal which they have found 'abandoned'. It usually turns out that the poor creature has been no more abandoned than a child left in a pram while its mother goes into a supermarket.

Our old roe deer arrived that way. She had been found 'abandoned' and taken to the R.S.P.C.A. who had neither the time nor the facilities to rear her. So she eventually landed up with me and I reared her on the bottle. That was eight years ago and she is still lying in the shade on the edge of the wood, contentedly chewing her cud. I never believed that she had really been abandoned. Roe deer habitually leave their kids

Feeding the orphan missel thrush

hidden in deep bracken while they are very young, and they only visit them to suckle them until they are strong enough to outrun their attackers. If the kind soul who had stumbled across her had left her where she was, the odds are a pound to a gooseberry that she would have been looked after better by her mother than by the most attentive human nursemaid.

The same thing happens with young birds. People see fledglings fresh from the nest and still unable to fly, so they pick them up and ask me what to do. My advice is always the same. I tell them to take them back where they found them and to put them down and watch what happens. Nine times of ten the young bird opens its beak and yells for food. Within seconds the old bird arrives, with a beakful of grubs to cram down the gaping maw and shut the youngster up. The most enthusiastic human can't compete with that.

Three weeks ago the headmistress of an infants' school rang me up to tell me that they had a young thrush and wanted to know what they must do to liberate it successfully. It would, of course, have been illegal to keep in an aviary a bird that had not been bred in captivity. It was almost impossible to advise her. Young birds which are easy enough to rear pose almost insuperable problems when the time comes to release them.

In the wild, the old birds will follow them around poking food into their beaks every time they open them for several days after they leave the nest. Then the young birds watch their parents catching caterpillars or whatever their natural food happens to be, and gradually learn to look after themselves by imitation. It is a facility denied to captive birds which often die of starvation long before they have learned to fend for themselves.

When I was a boy, it was common for the old Black Country bird fanciers to take fledgling song birds and put them under an ordinary garden riddle. The old birds heard their screams for food and poked it through the mesh of the riddle until the young were grown up enough to be imprisoned for their life sentence in a bird fancier's cage. It was a practice which I am glad to say has long been made illegal, but I wondered if it might not be possible to adapt the technique for helping orphan fledglings.

It so happens that when I was asked how to deal with this young thrush, there was a brood of wild thrushes just ready to leave their nest in our clematis. So I offered to collect the orphan and see what I could do. I thought that if I put him in a cage near the wild ones' nest, the old birds might very likely feed it. Then, when their brood left the nest, all I should have to do would be to liberate mine. It might then join his foster brothers to be reared and taught how to forage by the old birds.

Although I am convinced that it would have been an experiment which might well have succeeded, I am still no wiser whether it would have worked in this case for the simple reason that the stranger turned out to be a missel thrush and not a smaller common thrush at all. Missel thrushes are beautiful birds which Staffordshire folk called Storm cocks or Thrice cocks. They repeat their song three times and often herald bad weather, silhouetted against a thunderous sky from the top of the tallest tree. Some people believe that the biblical bird which crowed three times to signify St Peter's denial was no common rooster but a missel thrush.

Our wild thrushes took not the slightest notice, perhaps because they recognised no kinship, so I gave him the freedom of my study. For the first two weeks, I had to feed him entirely by hand, offering him raw meat, shredded to the shape of worms. Then I tried him on the maggots that fishermen use and he learned to peck at them instinctively when he saw them wriggle. I moved him to the shed outside, with peat on the floor and he gradually learned to find his own food amongst the loose litter in search of what I'd hidden.

The moment of truth really dawned when the time came for him to fend for himself. I fed him for the last time with shredded raw beef, encouraging him to pack his crop to bursting point. He seemed bloated enough to withstand a seige before the pangs of hunger overtook him. Then I opened the door and let him go. He disappeared into the oak trees at the edge of the wood, but within half an hour he came down to me and chirped around for food. I threw him some raw mince but he wasn't really hungry and went back into the wood.

Next morning, he came down again, fed and then followed me right to the wood when I took the dogs for a walk. He is still about, getting a little less tame and more self-reliant as each day passes. And the wilder he gets, the lovelier he looks, so that, with luck, he will thrive to herald the autumn storms and to charm his mate next spring, with one of nature's loveliest melodies.

# 5. Death of a deer

Few rural topics are more evocative than deer. Drop the word staghunting at a sophisticated cocktail party and the atmosphere will freeze until your gin requires no ice to chill it. Mention that a deer has been killed by a car and the prospective cures will range from preventive detention of motorists to corrugated roads that would stop a tank. Even the practical air of a country pub thickens with argument about protection and hunting and shooting.

If all the potential dangers to deer were fed into a computer, my bet is that the machine would hiccup over its decimal points and print a blank for the one that stared me in the face last week. My tame roe deer, Miss Roedoe, came to grief from the most unexpected cause.

Miss Roedoe, a family favourite

When she arrived nearly nine years ago, she was the most delightful sprite which ever ruled our household. She was only a few weeks old and had been found and taken to the R.S.P.C.A. in Midhurst, Surrey. I reared her on the bottle so that she grew up without knowing what fear is about. She was a friend of the dogs and often came for walks with them; she came to my study window for her biscuit at coffee time in the morning and lent grace to my friends by consenting to be photographed with them.

In return for the delight she gave me, I managed to provide surroundings that must be attractive to deer. She had woodland where she could lie-up in privacy, sweet clover and bramble and honey–suckle to browse – and occasionally my wife's roses when she managed to sneak into the garden.

The most important condition which deer prize above all riches, is a solid sense of security. This was possible because the fox-proof netting that kept her from straying into danger where she might be shot, also kept potential enemies out.

Everything seemed perfect until we wondered if she was lonely and hankering for the company of her own kind. She was always so spoiled that, once the notion had entered my mind, I couldn't rest until I had introduced a wild roe buck and his doe to join her. She wasn't impressed and would have no truck with them. They might have been foreign creatures of another race, but they settled down at once and proved their contentment by rearing kids of their own for four years out of five.

The first year the buck arrived, he chased the wild doe round in circles at rutting time till he caught her. He staked his claim to immortality by taking steps to ensure an heir the next year – and then chased her again to shorten the odds to a certainty. Roe bucks at rutting time always chase their does so continually in ritualistic patterns that they wear paths in the undergrowth as proof of their passion. Phlegmatic countrymen recognise these as doe rings. The more romantic believe that they are magic circles, made by moonlight when the fairies dance.

Miss Roedoe proved more nearly related to wallflowers than fairies, for the buck left her to sit out by herself. A year or so later his eye regained its bachelor glint. Familiarity had dulled the charms of his own mate and he cast errant eyes on our old doe. When he set off in pursuit, no outraged spinster could have panicked through the dark alleys of dockland with such determination. They went round the pool and through the wood and into the rushes time after time. She wasn't teasing him till his inhibitions fell apart. It was crystal clear that she meant to get away.

Thinking that I had done her no good turn by introducing this companion, I intervened and put her in another paddock out of reach. Things were never the same again. Their relationship had been frigid and stilted before, but after that the buck behaved as if *she* wasn't there. The wild group kept to themselves as a family and Miss Roedoe had to make do with the dogs and us for company.

Nine years old is a good age for a roe deer and she began to show signs of decline at about that age. Her eyes were not so bright nor her lovely coat so sleek. The 'clays' or separate cleaves of each foot splayed apart so that the slot between them was relatively wide. When she ran, she had an ungainly gait, as women do in skirts too narrow for their stride.

None of this would have mattered to us, for we shall all show signs of age if we live long enough. The snag was that the other roe deer don't see it in that light. They have no respect for senior citizens and suddenly took to bullying her. They gave her no peace when she lay down to chew her cud. The other doe came up and lowered her head, showing the white of her eyes. She didn't go as far as violence and it was just a threat display, but poor old Doe got up and hobbled off. Then the young doe followed her and repeated the performace until she got demoralised by the incessant nagging.

I had grown up indoctrinated by the idea that deer are graceful, noble creatures, persecuted by Man with his hounds and his gun. It had never occurred to me that they had any vice in them at all. It seemed quite unnatural that they could be cruel to each other, except perhaps in the short sharp battles at mating time.

This harrying of our old doe was the callous treatment of old age that one has come to expect of civilisation, but not of wild animals untainted by hypocrisy. I managed to cure it temporarily by allowing Doe into the paddock where the dogs run at night. And the vet came and filled her with injections and pills to restore her vitality which I helped by feeding concentrated rations.

She rallied for a while but the most skilled vet can't put back the clock. As her time grew closer, she took to lying in ever deeper and more secret thickets and, for some reason beyond my comprehension, the other deer ceased to bully her. They left her to die in peace and I found her curled-up where she had last slept.

She had lived to a great age for a roe deer, always eating well and sleeping free from fear of predators. It was all that a deer could ask but we missed her as much as if she'd been a favourite dog.

# 6. The early bird

Twenty years ago, I took part in a series of radio programmes called *Sunday Out*. The B.B.C. sent a team of four speakers for the weekend to a village pub somewhere in the Midlands and asked us to find our own amusement in the area. On Sunday evening a recording car turned up and the producer got us to talk about what we had done and who we had met. This was transmitted the following Friday night in the hopes that it might put ideas into the heads of whoever visited Uppingham or Ashby-de-la-Zouch, or wherever we had stayed the previous weekend.

The success of the programme depended on picking a friendly team with wide enough tastes to find something of interest for everyone. My friend, the late John Moore often rode his horse down the lanes and byways where we stayed. Geoffrey Bright, eminent auctioneer special-ised on local churches and stately homes and interesting snippets of architecture and history. Someone usually catered for motorists and cyclists and I was the chap who walked with his dog.

I don't know whether listeners enjoyed the programme, but I'm sure we did. It ran for a good many summer seasons and there was always keen competition to take part. We avoided the chromium-plated gin palaces which specialised in garlicky foreign food because our producer was a past master at picking little country pubs with the best beer and the most amusing local characters.

I spent happy Saturday evenings in the bar, chatting to keepers and poachers, cattle dealers and farmers. I made friends with a water diviner, a champion hedge layer and a woman who hunted her own pack of fox hounds. She had a wonderful plaster cornucopia with a saint over her front door – and another, with a figure of the devil, over the back! Although she hunted her own hounds, she had a tame fox which slept in her bedroom, which she claimed was perfectly safe if it met her pack of hounds.

My job in the programme was to tell listeners what there was to see if they happened to be interested in natural history. This is not always easy to do on a short visit to strange country so I always started work early on Sunday morning. Very early indeed.

There is so much dense cover in summer that cohorts of fascinating creatures might have skulked under my nose without being spotted. So I went out at first light when birds were singing or feeding or pecking for grit along the verges of country lanes. Rabbits and hares and deer were still out grazing in the open, and foxes and badgers returning from their night's prowl. That couple of hours before breakfast was worth the rest of the day to me. I often saw more than locals who had lived there for years but kept more respectable hours.

The same principle applies to our wood at home. When I get up early to feed the pigs and poultry, I take the dogs for a good walk before getting in for breakfast at about half-past eight or nine. The fact that I keep to the rides to avoid disturbance makes no difference because most woodland creatures will come out into the open provided they think it's safe. So it's comparatively rare for me to meet a beast or bird in our wood that I don't know almost personally.

This week has been a golden exception. A few weeks ago, we dammed a ditch to make a little pool. The result was far better than I expected. The only snag is that the water has risen two or three feet up the trunk of a hornbeam tree which I fear will 'drown' and die in consequence. Although I hate killing trees, I am not too worried about this one because it had already had its crown blasted out by lightning. As it dies, it will make a superb habitat for grubs and beetles which should prove irresistible to woodpeckers. A pair of waterhens built in the low branches almost before the pool had filled. Flamboyant dragonflies are breeding there already and wild duck flight in to feed at dawn and dusk.

The other morning, when out with the dogs, I was mooching quietly along the hedgerow towards the pool. I don't know what sixth sense sharpened my perception, but I was suddenly aware of a subtle thrill of anticipation without being able to pinpoint the cause. Normally it is the dogs which give prior warnings. My pointer Tick will slide forward, nostrils dilated so as not to squander the faintest whiff of promise. Or the lurchers, who rely more on sight than scent, grow visibly taller as they stand on tiptoe, intent on catching the first exciting glimpse. In either case, a sibilant whisper is all it takes to control them, so that they are assets rather than liabilities as companions on my walks.

Despite my premonitions, this time the dogs showed not the slightest interest as they approached the pool – and then I saw a flash of gaudy green that could only mean one thing. Stiffening into immobility, I hissed a command to 'drop'. Although the sound was so small, the dogs sensed the urgency and all four crouched at my feet as still as statues.

And there on a branch overhanging the pool, a kingfisher was sitting as still as we were. For a few seconds it seemed as if we were staring each other out. Then I realised he hadn't seen us. He was concentrating on prospecting for fish and cocked his head slightly before plopping into the water in a vertical dive. It was so clear that I could see him quite deep beneath the surface – and then he returned to his perch. As he shook himself dry, a shower of droplets rainbowed in the morning sun. The dogs were still unimpressed, so they had no temptation to disobey my command by moving. After what seemed minutes, the kingfisher broke the magic spell and darted away down the valley.

It is rare to get such reward for damming a sluggish ditch into a pool and it was worth all the self-discipline of rolling out of bed into the chill morning air. It was even more exciting than the pleasant surprise so common on those Sundays Out because such a bird on our land is worth more than two on somebody else's bushes.

# 7. Sleep to wake

I love spring for its snowdrops, its catkins, its bluebells and birdsong. I love to see the grass change from the withered gold of winter to the lush green of warmer days.

Its other marvels are less spectacular. Our pool at the moment is full of croaking frogs and toads, coupled in courtship and filling the shallows with spawn. A few weeks ago you could have gone over the place with a tooth comb and convinced yourself that some catastrophe had annihilated them all. All winter they have been in hibernation, triggered-off when the temperature fell to about eight degrees above freezing at the end of last year. They crept for safety into crevices in rocks or deep in the mud; into fissures in the earth or cellars or under fallen tree trunks.

For successful hibernation, the temperature should be as low and constant as possible without actually freezing. The reason for this is quite simple. All the bodily processes slow down as the temperature falls so that less and less energy is used up. It becomes unnecessary to eat and scarcely necessary to breathe. If the hiberation spot were not well enough insulated to prevent the temperature sinking to freezing, all warm-blooded animals would die and so would most cold-blooded animals too.

The term cold-blooded for such creatures as frogs and snakes is rather misleading. Their body simply takes on the temperature of their surroundings, and the colder they are, short of freezing, the more their whole metabolism slows up. As they grow warmer, they become more active until they reach a critical point beyond which it would be as dangerous for them as being too cold.

So their instinct drives them to seek cool, but not freezing, spots to hibernate in winter and to migrate to pools to spawn in spring. They need spots warm enough in summer to raise their energy to its optimum for catching food to lay on fat for winter, but never so warm that their systems cannot cope.

Birds get over the hardships of winter by migrating to more suitable climates but animals which are not equipped to travel great distances need more complicated mechanisms to hibernate successfully. Hedgehogs and dormice are past masters in the art of insulation. They build hibernation nests of moss and leaves and scraps of vegetation that would make our most expensive eiderdowns seem as crude as hair shirts. It is as important for them to slow down their body processes as it is for frogs and snakes, but they have an added complication. Like us, they are warm-blooded and their bodies carry an in-built thermostat which tries to maintain their blood temperature constant. If we keep still in a very cold place our body uses up energy in trying to keep its blood temperature up to normal. This would make it physically impossible for us to hibernate. We should use up too much energy. We could not replace this by eating or drinking because our sleep would be too deep.

Hedgehogs and dormice get over this by making a nest so well insulated that their temperature does not fall too far. There is a wonderful mechanism in hibernating animals which changes the chemistry of the blood so that they become virtually cold-blooded. Their respiration rate slows right down to perhaps a breath in five minutes and life almost comes to a halt.

Scientists who have been studying the hibernation of bats for years have done a great deal of work on the Greater Horseshoe bat which lives in caves. It hangs from the roof so it cannot make use of a thermostatically-controlled nest, as dormice and hedgehogs do. Nor can it maintain relatively constant temperature below ground which serves frogs and toads so well.

Bats must choose a place to hang and hibernate which is as cold as possible without freezing. Caves which have two or more entrances, and therefore a current of air, fall in temperature as fast as outside temperature falls. So these bats choose this type of cave to start the winter. The snag is that when it gets really cold, the air would freeze and so would the bats. As the temperature falls, the bats sink deeper into sleep. They become completely unconscious a few degrees above freezing and could logically be expected to die in deep sleep if conditions got any worse.

Instead of that, when once the critical point is reached, the bats wake up and fly to another cave. Nobody knows how this happens because the theory that the blood chemistry changes to make them cold-blooded should keep them as warm or cold as the surrounding air. This time, the bats choose a cave with only one entrance, where the temperature stays the same in summer as winter because the air cannot circulate. It remains at about 12 degrees above freezing.

"Very clever," you might think, "but if they had had human scientists to advise them, they might have hibernated there first and avoided the perils of flying from one cave to another." It wouldn't have worked because it isn't cold enough to induce what amounts to suspended animation. Instead of breathing once in five minutes, they might breathe once in two. That would produce enough waste products to force them to excrete which, in turn, would make them use enough energy to make it necessary to fly out and catch food.

It is a chain reaction which could prove fatal in weather cold enough to make food hard to find. So bottle caves can only be used as temporary sanctuaries. For the rest of winter, they must hibernate in conditions which are only a hair's breadth from death. When spring comes, their reappearance may not be as dramatic as a primrose, but it is a most miraculous resurrection.

# 8. "Love me, love my dog"

Strangers stop me in the street because they recognise my dog. She is the German short-haired pointer which has shared my life since she was a tiny pup. I called her Tick because of the liver-ticked marking on her roan coat. People remember her for her performances on television. I always take it as a compliment and bask in the reflected glory because a well-behaved dog is usually the product of a sensible relationship between animal and man.

I have often been known by my dogs. For years I was referred to as " 'im as belongs the lemon-eyed bitch", because my lemon and white Stafford bull terrier, Rebel, became a legend for the number of rats she killed. We went ferreting every Sunday morning for years and turned up whenever we could to catch the rats uncovered when they were

Tick, the German short-haired pointer

threshing a rick. Her prowess was such that she killed over a hundred in a day several times.

When she went, my lurcher bitch, Gipsy, made as good a reputation even among true-blooded gypsies brought up with such dogs to fill the pot with the rabbits and hares. My alsatian, Tough, was loved by some and respected by all.

I am a disciple of the creed that handsome is as handsome does. I always try to get a dog bred for brains and stamina and work, instead of the empty-headed good looks so often seen at dog shows. I believe that if my dog is intelligent enough, it will be nobody's fault but mine if she doesn't do me credit. And I have been simply delighted with the progress of my pointer puppy, Tick.

Professional dog trainers usually like to start work on a young dog at about nine months old. They let it run wild till then, romping with other young dogs for exercise in a boisterous group that chucks discipline out of the window. It comes as a pretty rude shock to such puppies when they wake up on the business end of a lead and are shown what happens to unruly dogs who fail to observe rules they didn't even know existed.

I trained Tick with Indian corn and chocolate drops. Instead of starting when she had acquired natural bad habits, I tried to prevent their development, nipping the first signs of chasing ducks or deer or poultry in the bud. That was where the Indian corn came in. Each golden grain was the size of a garden pea and twice as hard and heavy. The moment the thought of chasing crossed her mind, I deluged her with a shower of corn which caused no pain but distracted her attention. Then I walked away and she followed before she even remembered what evil designs had occupied her mind a moment earlier.

I taught her to come when I called, largely by going on strange ground as much as possible. All young things crave for a sense of security and are afraid of being lost on their own. And she soon learned that if she ignored requests to come, I disappeared as if by magic.

Having taught her what she might not do, I set about the more positive side of her training. She is as passionately fond of chocolate as most dogs, and would do anything for a quarter of chocolate drops. I taught her to sit on command, lie down, bark when told to speak and walk at heel by a series of sweet bribes and rewards when she pleased me. As a result, obedience was a reflex action for her long before most pups started training. And she never faced the discomforts of unlearning bad habits.

She more than paid the confectioner's bill by her first appearance on television's Animal Magic, when we made a short film of her early training, performing with such verve that she was immediately invited for a second appearance. We both found this even more fun because we took a film camera man on a walk, choosing a route to show autumn colours.

We started on Cannock Chase in time to see the rising sun, red-eyed and bleary through the morning mist. As the dew washed the sleep from his eyes, he came up like a halo over the trees, painting the leaves in rich red tints. After a couple of hours, we had a monumental fry-up for breakfast at a lorry drivers' 'caff' and moved on to the landscaped park and cultivated fields of a great estate.

The head keeper is an old friend and I would never have heard the last of it if my pup had let me down. But she walked steadily as an old dog through a herd of park deer and refused to be panicked by a wheeling herd of playful ponies. She pointed at sitting pheasants but never disturbed them; ignored a pair of swans and showed us where duck and partridges hid.

Not only is she a delightful companion for a country walk, but it is a pleasure to work in any film where she has the leading role.

# 9. Island of enchantment

A few years ago I hired a bulldozer and scooped out quite a wide channel along one side of the pool to leave an island ten to fifteen yards from the shore. This was not the extravagence it might sound because I would rather spend what might have been holiday money on something around the place. I hope it will still be giving me pleasure when the bikini girls on some crowded beach have long grown fat and gross.

I caused my island to be made partly to improve the view from the house, to give the pool a more rounded and aesthetic air, and to show up the reflection of the oak tree in the evening light. I also thought it would make an attractive site for nesting birds. When it was done and had time to grow a gown of weeds and grass to clothe its muddy chastity, it looked alluring from the house. Whatever the wind, there are ripples on one side and calm on the other. On the stillest summer night when the breeze hasn't the strength to stir the water, the ducks make ever changing patterns as they come and go.

The first practical excitement was the arrival of a pair of Canada geese. Three years ago, a lady from Wokingham had brought a pet Canada goose for me to liberate because she feared he would get shot at home. He settled down to fend for himself and flew off in the autumn when wild Canada geese begin to flock.

When a pair arrived the first spring after the island was made I was delighted for two reasons. I was glad the hand-reared gosling had survived and paired and hoped they would stay with me to nest. There was no proof of course that either of these visitors was the Wokingham gosling. I am not in favour of ringing birds except for very special reasons, so I had placed no positive means of identification round his leg. But one was so tame that it seemed quite likely to have been a hand-reared bird. They settled on the pool and made their headquarters on the south bank of the island, simply watching for hour after hour what went on. There can hardly have been a mouse stirring in the paddock or surrounding woodland that those birds didn't know about. There is nothing unusual about this. Wild birds take as much trouble where they build their nests as how.

When I was young I used to find a great many birds' nests by patience and luck. As I grew older, my previous experience gradually narrowed my searches because it taught me the sort of places to look. Then I discovered that an hour standing still as a log, simply watching the movements of birds returning to nests or coming off to feed, was worth two hours' haphazard search.

A refinement to that was the knowledge that birds are ruled by the clock as surely as commuters catching their morning train. They feed at the same time each day, dust bath in the same place and sun themselves when the shadows clear their favourite bathing spot. Now I enjoy trying to analyse not just what they do, but the reason why. This pair of Canada geese settled on our island and were obviously prepared to spend time watching and waiting to establish what hazards they might have to face. It is a species that chooses to nest on an island if possible, even if the island is in a pool no bigger than a tennis court. When the female is sitting tight on eggs, she is less likely to have her head bitten off by a prowling fox if a strip of water bars his way. She is less likely to have eggs stolen by small boys if the expedition entails a swim in icy water in the spring. And the goslings will be safer, from prowling cats and stoats. It would be as stupid for geese to choose a building site subject to flooding by a rising river after every storm as it would be for you or I to build in the path of an approaching motorway.

Our visitors must have satisfied themselves on all counts. Or all but one! The island is never disturbed, expect perhaps by crows. There is a fox-proof fence round the whole place which keeps out trespassers as well as vermin. The grazing in the paddock is short and sweet and augmented by grain I throw down for the ducks. The water doesn't rise or fall and there is enough privacy in the reeds for a comfortable nest. Just as the goose was coming up into condition to lay, the danger they had overlooked arrived. It was another pair of Canada geese.

They are gregarious birds that flock in friendly herds except in the breeding season when they are exceptionally territorial. So territorial that the new arrivals proved to be the worst sort of dogs in the manger. They had nested for several years on a small island in a pool half a mile away but came to my pool daily to feed and preen their feathers.

The pair they found on our new island were obviously unacceptable as neighbours and the gander gave them no peace at all. He kept flying at them and driving them unmercifully until they went to find another nesting site. Then he hadn't even the grace to take our island over but left it untenanted.

This year I'm hoping for better things. 'Our' pair of geese have been here for a week. I think that if they really get settled down before the old pair arrive, the gander may be mature and strong enough to see the others off instead of slinking away himself. But whatever happens, my study window will be as good as the pound seats for seeing the drama unfold.

# 10. Lock up the loyal guards

Your childhood, like mine, was probably stuffed with stories about the unselfish devotion of sheep dogs guarding their flocks. If you fumble in the secret recesses of your sub-conscious mind, you may recall sagas of courage and initiative where dogs risked death searching in snowdrifts, or battling with wolves, for the lives of their sheep.

So dog lovers may get a nasty shock to discover that the motives of sheepdogs are not as pure as they may seem. Forget for the moment any preconceived ideas you may have about intuitive bonds between master and dog and consider, instead, the skill of a trainer who can persuade his dog to go right or left by whistle when he is two hundred yards away.

If you have a reasonably trained dog of your own, it may not seem miraculous that the shepherd can call his dog from a distance when he whistles. But try training your dog to go away from you on command in the precise direction that you require. You will find that a far stiffer test of control. But it isn't the sheepdog's capacity to learn that I am calling in question, for only a fool would doubt that.

Training a dog to this pitch is not just a matter of teaching him tricks unrelated to his natural instinct, like animals in a circus. Training sheepdogs is more a question of channelling and directing their natural instincts.

If you watch dogs at a sheepdog trial, you will see what I mean. The sheep to be penned start off as part of a flock several hundred yards away from the shepherd who has the dog sitting quietly by him. He is quivering with excitement, straining against his master's will to go, every bit as hard as if he was physically fastened by collar and lead. The least sign sets him off towards the sheep as keen as a whippet after a rabbit. When he has almost reached the sheep, one long whistle from his master drops him in his stride as effectively as if he had been shot. This takes long and patient training.

The shepherd watches the sheep and he 'works' his dog to right or left by the remote control of his whistle until the moment comes to split off the fragment he wants from the flock. This is called 'shedding' the sheep. At a sign, the dog dives in among them, cutting out the exact group his master wills and he herds them back towards him. That is the bit to watch. If the sheep are awkward or stubborn, as sheep so often are, the dog may lose his patience and go in close, nipping them as he passes to convince them that he means business.

Such nips are no love-bites, no paternal hints. They are just to restore discipline to its civilised place in canine priorities. He doesn't really want to guard the flock. He wants to savage it and eat it. All civilisation is no more than scratch deep and only the control of the shepherd and the hereditary habits of generations of selective breeding avert catastrophe. Some dogs let their enthusiasm run away with their self control till they grow too 'hard' for work with sheep and have to be downgraded to cattle dogs, or destroyed.

The very best are those who walk the tightrope between guardians and predators and are prevented from attacking only by force of habit and the strength of will of their masters. These dogs are fast and showy and tirelessly keen. They play an endless charade, leading themselves up the garden of desire to kill, but sheathing their fangs at the last instant.

All that the spectator then sees is a brilliant dog running endless ritual circles round his charges, to divide and herd and pen them as if he loved them tenderly. It is a superb exhibition of man's ingenuity in selective breeding and patient training to harness aggressive instincts in the cause of peace. It is a lesson we might learn with profit ourselves.

The snag is that civilised habits so easily revert to the instincts from which they were fashioned. Sheepdogs have been selectively bred to show high intelligence so that they are easy to train. This exceptional intelligence is close akin to cunning so that the brainiest sheepdog may yearn for a Jekyll and Hyde life and be bright enough to achieve it without getting caught. He may spend his days delighting crowds with exhibitions of his skill at minding sheep. Then, when he has deceived everyone that he could harbour no evil thoughts towards anything in a cloak of wool, he may sneak out at night to feast on mutton.

The most likely time of year for him to try is when ewes are lambing and are at their most vulnerable, with the carnal smells of birth and death and helpless infancy to goad on hunters with supreme temptation. Dogs raiding flocks are always news; as predictable as pretty girls with cuddly lambs and daffodils and snowdrops.

Farmers and shepherds have no illusions about their sheepdogs. They know that, without cast iron discipline, the most worthy will degenerate into hoodlums. So the wise ones shut their dogs up at night – and guard their flocks into the bargain. Country dogs are just not let loose at night when lambs are about and most of the damage is caused by packs of dogs roaming unchecked from the edge of towns. Farmers and shepherds wait for them with guns but, even so, some get through the defences.

It is hard on the dogs and I don't blame them because it is their nature. It is even harder on the sheep. The fault lies with dog owners who want pleasure and companionship but who accept no responsibility in return.

# 11. Why the herons blush

Herons and I have evolved a complicated love-hate relationship that would bamfoozle a psychologist. I go to extreme lengths to preserve them – but they pay me nothing back. I am prepared to patrol from dawn to dusk with a rifle on the off-chance of picking off one of their enemies which dares to cast so much as a beady eye in their direction. I deny myself the pleasure of going in 'their' part of the wood when they want privacy for their nuptials, though in law it is not theirs, but mine. And I am aggressively rude to trespassers in the heronry. I even grumble at good neighbours who use firearms to defend their expensive fishing from my feathered vandals.

The dignified heron

The only measures of my success are the dull statistics of their population which has quadrupled in the seven years we have shared the same wood. But I am the first to admit their imperfections. They are such cowardly birds that even an inoffensive waterhen can drive them off if she thinks they have designs on her chicks. They owe their success to sly subterfuge and catch frogs and fish and voles and moles by standing statuesque for hours till some unwary creature wanders within range of their rapier beaks. The herons do not even draw the line at fratricide. When food is scarce or the old birds are killed, it is not uncommon for the strongest young in the nest to turn on their weaker brothers and sisters and eat them up.

But even the lack of rosy tinted spectacles to examine their faults does not blind me to their attractions. No grey is softer or more subtle than herons' wings, no yellow eyes so bright.

Groups of herons assembling to pair and nest in earliest spring are among the first birds to herald winter's waning, and they perform a ritual courtship dance that I rate as exciting as the lekking of blackcock. Blackcock gather in traditional lekking areas, often while the snow is still on the ground, and warm themselves into an amorous frenzy with the repeated chases of mock-battle.

Heron are more dignified. They sit hunched in dejected groups as if the most glamorous female would be impotent to arouse their passions. A new arrival passes down the whole line in a series of slow hops and skips that often inspire the others to take a few desultory steps, as if they would all join in. This proves to be no more than a symbolic acknowledgement of the ritual, for they subside into their dignified stances and their ardour flags before the instinct that inspired it has time to swell to passion. They are such shy and persecuted birds that most people see no more of them than great grey silhouettes flapping slowly across the sky at dawn or dusk, or hunched at the water's edge waiting for fish.

It is my privilege to know them more intimately. This year there were fifty-eight nests in the wood behind our house and before they laid their eggs, they collected on their gathering ground. Wild horses wouldn't drag its exact location from me, lest strangers intruded and disturbed the birds next year. When I have watched their dance, I spy on the most intimate secrets of the rest of their courtship from a distance through my binoculars.

Believe it or not, I see them blush. It is not the blush of modest Victorian maids, who would have swooned in our permissive age. Herons go scarlet with passion. Their bills and eyes turn fiery and even their long green legs go orange splashed with red. This blushing is so transient that it lasts only as long as their ecstasy and is quite different from the colour changes of other birds that moult into bright breeding plumage.

When I found a young heron the other day too weak to stand, my instinct was to help. Perhaps his parents had been shot or simply gone off selfishly and abandoned him. When I saw him first, he was wandering disconsolately round my pool with no apparent ideas of how to fish. Next day he took no notice till I was within five yards and the day after that he was so weak with hunger that he let me pick him up.

I fed him by force for a few days with slivers of liver dipped in raw egg to make it slide down more easily. Some gauge of my success was his rapidly growing strength and the fact that he soon learned to pick up the meat for himself. When I let him go, he was strong enough to fly and, I hope, to fend for himself. Not that he showed any gratitude. He demonstrated his independence by jabbing me with his spike of a bill and ripping at my flesh to prove that he felt under no obligation.

Perhaps some psychologist can tell me why I suffered him with masochistic apathy instead of wringing his neck as more practical folk might have done.

# 12. Jelly babies

When I was a kid there was no television and even the wireless was no more than a crackly cacophony. Gruff 'uncles' and squeaky 'aunties' jollied us on in Children's Hour programmes designed to improve our minds. It was a solitary entertainment filtering into our private ears through headphones which had not acquired enough volume to annoy the rest of the family. Pop music and loudspeakers had yet to intrude into private homes. Our amusements were home-made. Spinning tops and bowling hoops were our pastimes, each with its own specific season.

As an only child, with no fondness for team games, I preferred bird-nesting and butterfly collecting to cricket, and ferreting to football. At the turn of the year, I got a kick from finding the first batch of frog spawn in a pit-hole at the back of the house. I always brought a jam-jar full of it back home and stuck it in my bedroom window to watch the tadpoles form, though my ignorance was such that I lost most of them. I got more kicks from rearing the survivors than if I'd been invited to play in the 1st XI. Most of my school mates reckoned frog spawn as revolting as the school sago pudding it so resembled but it made up in interest for me what it lacked in beauty!

Each female frog is capable of laying in excess of five thousand eggs and a mass of spawn that size would fill a fair-sized bucket. I was curious how so small a creature emitted such bulk. The female frog ejects black eggs in a jet as dense as treacle which sinks to the bottom of the pool, and if the male frog doesn't fertilise them within a few seconds, he is too late.

They absorb water as they drop, and swell into the familiar mass of translucent jelly which encases the inky dots that will develop into tadpoles. This jelly contains as much as 99.5 per cent of water, and it has all the properties of water – except that it is solid. Because it is solid, there are no convection currents and, because the eggs are black, they do not reflect light but absorb it. As a result, the eggs are from half a degree to two degrees centigrade warmer than the surrounding pool, which helps them to hatch. The higher temperature is also vital in the bitter cold of early spring because the water temperature may freeze until it is actually lethal. The frogs usually spawn in shallow pools, but in any case the spawn is slightly lighter than pure water so that it floats.

No decent school gaffer fails to fire his pupils' imagination with classroom demonstrations of tadpoles developing from inky dots to perfect miniature frogs, and most people have watched the process with varying degrees of interest. My master was always game for a spot of oneupmanship so he tried to show us something the others hadn't seen. His latest toy was a very advanced microscope which was the apple of his eye, so he gave us a demonstration of his expertise.

He took a dozen tadpoles, about as big as peas, and operated on each under his microscope. I was always more attentive of what he did than what he said but, so far as I remember, he said it was a thyroid gland he removed from each. He predicted that the tadpoles would continue to grow – but not to develop. Sure enough, they grew as big as marbles, then as big as walnuts, but showed no signs of changing into frogs.

When they stopped growing they still had tadpole tails, no legs and tiny eyes and mouths, in spite of the fact that they were as big as frogs. Then he fed them thyroid extract, the gland he had dissected out, and sure enough, they turned from giant tadpoles to normal-sized frogs.

If he did it now, I should deprecate it as a pointless experiment because as I mature with age I dislike more and more experiments on animals simply for the sake of knowledge. But that experiment certainly had its effect. I may not even be certain which gland he removed, but it did drive home the lesson of what a lot there is to learn. A couple of years as a biology student gave me a sickening of dissecting frogs myself, and for years I never wanted to look another in the eye, either alive or dead.

But I can remember they were so common that they were jumping around in the garden after every other shower of rain, and nobody gave them a second thought. Now they are so scarce that, when I found one in the yard the other night, I picked it up and carried it to the safety of the pool lest anything should harm it before it had time to spawn.

Frogs normally hibernate in mud, often some distance from their breeding pools, and it is wonderful how they survive so long out of direct contact with air. Their way of breathing is their secret. They don't have ribs so that they get their main intake of air by pulsating their throats which draws air in like bellows. But they can also breathe under water through their skin. Although this isn't so efficient, they can absorb enough oxygen through their skin to keep them going at the reduced pace of living needed during hibernation.

Their numbers have really declined mainly through the filling-in of little ponds where they bred successfully and because of poisonous pesticides getting into ditches and streams. So we made two new pools, both filled by pure water draining from the wood. There was spawn in the one in Primrose Dell last year and I am trying to make the newer one attractive by planting it with pond weeds.

This year I have shed off a few years to go frog spawning again. If I introduce enough spawn into my new pool to get a decent crop of tadpoles, we should have a thriving colony of breeding frogs when traditional pools are drying up.

# 13. Enter Fred

Last week I was done a good turn . . . by a cat! This inadvertent feline favour was unexpected because cats do so much damage to small birds that I have no great affection for them.

A cat had caught an unfledged barn owl in November at a farm in Warwickshire. It had apparently fallen from its nest in the rafters of the barn and was so young that its baby down had not yet been replaced by feathers. The farmer's son had reared it by hand in the kitchen and it grew up so tame that it answered to the name of Fred and flew in and out of the window as it liked to the world outside. As it moulted into adult plummage, enough grey feathers appeared on its beautiful buff back to suggest that Fredrika might have been a more appropriate name.

The chances are, I think, that Fred will turn out to be a hen and the theory is strengthened by the fact that it was not only her feathers she changed when she moulted. She underwent a predictable feminine change of mind. I am not suggesting that she remembered her traumatic experience when she fell out of the nest and was caught by the cat. She was far too young for that.

Although she ignored the house cat which shared the kitchen while she was being reared, it seems that she was only biding her time. As she grew up, her hooked bill acquired the power of a pair of nut crackers and her talons developed the grip of a vice lined with surgical needles. The rhyme about the owl and the pussy cat going to sea together proved to be as far-fetched nonsense as its title implied. Far from sharing her honey – or anything else – wrapped up in a five pound note, Fred sailed down from the kitchen shelf with daggers drawn at the first sign of a pussy cat's whisker round the door. The cat retired in disorder and the farmer felt a twinge of sympathy.

When he heard from a mutual friend that I harboured a hitherto unrequited yearning for a barn owl, I was invited to call and collect Fred.

Barn owls are among our most heavily protected species and it is illegal to harm or even disturb them in any way. It is even illegal to

Fred the barn owl in her new home

photograph them at nest without a permit from the Nature Conservancy. The reason they are becoming so rare is because so many have caught and eaten rats and mice which were dying from poison, put down either by pest destruction officers for rats, or by farmers on dressed corn. There are also a few gamekeepers and sportsmen so ignorant that they still slaughter anything with a hooked bill, in spite of the fact that barn owls are among farmers' best friends, past masters at killing rats and mice. Because they are so persecuted and in real danger of extinction, it is rightly almost impossible to acquire one legally.

Fred was an exception. If she hadn't been rescued from the cat, she would have been eaten. I promised that if she came to me, I would try to give her the best of all worlds. I would give her her freedom – but persuade her, if possible, to settle where I could watch over her safety while giving myself the pleasure of watching her regularly and learning more about the habits of barn owls.

When I arrived at the farm, I was delighted to discover how tame and healthy Fred was. She was sitting on a pile of newspapers by the kitchen stove, free to come and go when and where she liked. She was so tame that she never so much as ruffled a feather at the sight of two strangers when the photographer and I walked in. She posed on her owner's shoulder to say Hello to me and Goodbye to him. She sat among the pots and pans and on the washing machine. As a bonus, she showed just what she thought of cats when one stupidly walked through the door.

I learned that her main diet had been wood pigeon, which would be no problem for me – and that, although she would put up with strangers and hazards, her pet hate was the sound of a vacuum cleaner. This endeared her to me greatly because there are few sounds I loathe more, and one of my habitual grumbles to my wife is that it would be easier to concentrate in a factory press shop than in my study when our clean home is being sucked even cleaner.

Some of the difficulties I had taken on began to filter through my enthusiasm almost before Fred and I got home. Superficially everything was all right because she took to the dogs like old friends and settled down on a shelf in my study. But I have no intention of keeping her confined a moment longer than it takes to get her self-supporting and accustomed to her new home. I want to establish her somewhere desirable enough for her to attract a male and breed a brood. My idea is to build an owl cote in the highest gable of the outbuildings and to erect a temporary aviary outside. I can keep her confined here at night till she knows the surroundings well enough to return to be hand fed by me until she is ready for me to set her free.

Meanwhile I plan to let her sleep and doze through the hours of daylight on the shelf in my study so that she stays accustomed to the sights and sounds of human beings. This is because I don't want her to return to the wild too soon in case she is unsuccessful at catching her own food. She might well starve if she was not confident enough to return to be hand fed by me.

It was obvious at once that all this is harder in practice than it sounds as a theory. Fred has been reared on wood pigeon and fed freely as soon as I produced one. But she showed no interest either in dead mice or sparrows – and if she escaped she could catch mice but not pigeons. So I have been as busy catching mice and sparrows as an old-fashioned rat catcher or she-cat with kittens. I have got to persuade Fred to develop a palate for mice. And then I've got to teach her to catch them by covering her aviary with leaves like a woodland floor. I shall have to tie a bit of cotton on a dead mouse and play hard-to-get by snatching it away every time Fred makes a pounce.

I hope that I shall eventually arouse her hunting instincts so that I shall be able to set her free in May or June at the height of the crop of young mice and voles, which are easy to catch. Only when our partnership has reached this point will it be safe to take down the bars from her aviary in reasonable confidence that my share of the bargain will be a pair of beautiful barn owls living free about the place.

But I've long discovered that nothing worthwhile is easy.

# 14. Born free?

A few weeks ago I bought a bunch of pigs with curly tails. This may cause no surprise to those who remember the chubby piggies of their childhood story books, but they might be shocked to learn how many modern pigs have no tails at all, or only amputated stumps. The cause of this deformity is the conditions under which they have to live.

Fattening units often consist of rows of narrow pens with a corridor along one end. There is a chain, bright and polished at one end, dangling into each pen. The most casual observer would appreciate that these fattening units are labour-saving miracles compared to old-fashioned pigsties. There is no water to carry, no back-breaking barrows of pig muck to cart. The unit is air-conditioned and the humidity

The animated cultivators at work

and temperature are controlled so that the heat given off by the pigs'
bodies keep the whole place at the theoretically ideal temperature.

It isn't even necessary to give them straw bedding to keep them
warm. Pigs are naturally clean animals and empty themselves as far as
possible from where they eat. So, in theory, they sleep on the concrete,
which is smoother and more comfortable than the perforated dung-pit
by the water trough. This is very convenient for the pig-man who can
walk along the passage tipping measured quantities of fattening food on
the clean concrete where the pigs sleep.

Or on to the part of concrete which is supposed to be clean. A minor
snag is that not every pig is bright enough to realise that the end of the
pen with the holes in the floor was put there by a man who studied super
pigs. Although the low-brow pigs may be house-trained by nature, they
get confused about which end of the unit they are supposed to use. So
they often soil the patch which was allocated for dining and relaxation.

If it was not for such inconsiderate misfits who make sleeping and
eating a misery for their fastidious fellows, such scientifically designed
fattening units might be more successful.

You might be wondering what the dangling chains are for. The scientists had overlooked one thing. Boredom. Most animals, including pigs,
were created to work for their living. They have to expend a great deal
of energy, in the wild, to find the food they need. When they are confined to close quarters, in an unnatural welfare state, they get bored, as
human vandals do. In an effort to break the monotony, one imaginative
pig thinks what fun it would be to tweak his fellow's tail. The squeal it
evokes livens up the whole party so that, in no time at all, they are all at
it. Soon there are pigs with amputated stumps or no tails at all.

The first solution the scientists tried was to darken the units so the
pigs couldn't see each others' tails. The lights were only turned on at
feeding time. Such gloom did help but it wasn't the complete answer.
So they hung up the chains which the pigs now bite until they shine and
rattle to pass away their time. But it doesn't stop them biting tails as
well.

Some pig breeders defend this because it is intensive husbandry.
They say that it is necessary because labour is so expensive and there
are starving human mouths to fill. They claim it isn't cruel or the pigs

would pine and not wax fat. Their opponents call it factory farming and think that the money would be better spent on birth control of the human population explosion.

Whoever is right in theory, I do not believe that this particular form of exploitation is justified in practice. I mentioned that the bunch of pigs that I bought had curly tails. They had been born in open fields and the man who bred them believes in keeping as close as he can to Nature. When he has weaned his piglets, he fattens them in open fold yards where they have plenty of room to move in God's fresh air and daylight. He thinks that they may grow more slowly than intensively kept pigs, but that his lower losses from disease more than compensate him. And he can look himself in the eye when he is shaving without fearing his own barbarities will jog his razor.

Before some boffin bleats that such old-fashioned husbandry will soon send him up the spout, I would add that he produces over a hundred pigs a week and farms a thousand acres. If he is in financial straits, he conceals it very well.

I wanted some pigs to do some work for me. There are large patches of bracken in our wood, too dense for seedling trees to grow, too thick and wet to be much use to wildlife. If I could clear some of these patches and leave a tilth of soil exposed in autumn when the seeds are falling, I might get a crop of natural regenerated woodland.

So I fenced off half an acre as an experiment, put a shelter in it, and bought ten pedigree saddle back pigs from my farmer friend. It is a joy to watch them because what is work to me is pleasure to them. Their powerful snouts grub up the soil in search of succulent roots and bulbs and insects. They browse the birch leaves and crop the grass and sunbathe in luxury when they grow weary. At night or when it rains too hard, they huddle on dry straw in a comfortable heap in the shelter I built for them.

They don't need much looking after – and no cleaning out, for they enrich the soil with dung as they turn it over. All I do is take them a barrel of fresh water on the tractor every other day and scatter pig nuts for them when I feed the poultry. Perhaps they won't grow as fast as their relatives in intensive units, but they find a lot of their own food so that they don't cost as much to keep.

I am no slushy sentimentalist and I look forward to superb pork and home-cured ham and bacon in due course. My conscience will not trouble me because my home-fed pigs will have suffered no injuries from their fellows, nor horrors at the hand of Man. At least they will prevent their appetites being depraved by boredom.

# 15. Against the odds

A stranger rang me the other day from somewhere north of Derby. She said two badger cubs had arrived at her back door under their own steam and she didn't know what to do about them. Would I like them? she asked. My answer was a categoric *No*! This was not because I am not fond of badgers. I have worked closely with them for more than twenty years and I doubt if anyone is keener on their welfare than I am.

I declined for the simple reason that my own sow badger, which I reared on the bottle in 1968, would probably kill them as soon as they were strong enough to get around on their own. She is living free in the wood but still calls every night at the house for tit-bits. If she had spared the strange cubs' lives, I am sure that they would have stood no chance when they trespassed into the territory of the many wild badgers that live around here.

I wondered how the cubs had arrived on her doorstep. Their mother had probably been trapped or snared or poisoned or run over. When she failed to return to suckle her litter, they would eventually be forced by starvation to go out in search of her. The fact that they were screaming and chattering with hunger lends colour to the theory.

Badger cubs are tough and there would have been no difficulty about hand-rearing them. The snag is what to do with them when they are weaned. Setting them free in the woods so that they can 'return' to the wild is all right only for those who never grieve about what their eyes don't see. The brutal fact is that turning young badgers down is almost inevitably sentencing them to an excrutiating painful death. They would be attacked by wild badgers which would mutilate them terribly, as I discovered when I rescued my own young boar just in the nick of time. For the next eight days he lay between life and death.

The alternative is to keep them as pets in a cage. They are nocturnal and will give their owners little pleasure by day. They are so full of energy when they wake that they will dig and tear for hour after hour, night after night, in a futile bid for freedom. A few specialist naturalists have rehabilitated young badgers successfully as my own sow can testify. But I can't repeat it while she is still here to defend her territory.

So I explained to the woman from Derbyshire that the usual alternative for tame badgers is the agony of execution by wild badgers or a sentence of imprisonment for life. I felt she would be kinder to take her cubs to the vet and ask him to destroy them. The harsh fact is that the odds against survival for most wild creatures are enormous.

A pair of badgers have three or four cubs a year and may breed for about eight seasons. So each pair could produce over twenty young in a lifetime. If more than two or three lived, the badger population would increase. It doesn't need a computer to calculate that the odds against their survival are around ten to one. The same applies to most wild creatures. The blackbirds and thrushes that nest in most gardens could rear two broods of four fledglings for three or fours years running. If I were a gambling man, I would be prepared to lay twenty-eight to one against any one of them lasting his allotted span. Wrens and tits, which have enormous broods, have less chance still. The surplus is really hatched as food for other creatures.

Although they have few wild enemies, fox cubs are among the commonest victims of misplaced kindness at this time of year. As they grow up, the vixen is driven almost frantic in her efforts to keep pace with their insatiable appetites. Her maternal instinct forces her to drop her caution and take stupid risks, hunting by day and taking poultry and game under the aggrieved noses of farmers and keepers. So more vixens are shot and snared when they are feeding cubs than at any time of the year. And the cubs are dug out by men with terriers who often decide that they are too innocent to kill and give them to children as pets.

Perhaps, unfortunately, they have more chance of survival than young badgers if turned out in woodland at about six months old. I say unfortunately because a hungry cub which has lost his fear of man by being reared in captivity can do untold harm. Because his cunning has been blunted, he may be careless enough to get caught in the act, which will give his wild relatives an unnecessarily bad name.

Some of the weakest and most attractive creatures seem to be the most vulnerable. Baby hares – or leverets – are about the most defenceless creatures imaginable for the first few days of their lives. They are born fully furred, with eyes open. But they are not hidden in a hole as young rabbits are, but left in a tuft of grass or a clump of nettles in the open. Sometimes they are even dropped on bare ploughland. Rats, crows, cats, stoats or foxes, whatever predator one can think of, must find them easy meat. In theory if not in practice.

Last week I noticed a crow 'dive-bombing' a clump of grass in the field next to our house. Every time he swooped, a hare – I imagine a nursing doe – rushed out at him and drove him off. One never thinks of 'timid' hares as brave, but that crow certainly didn't want to mix it, so he fetched up his mate. One dived to decoy the hare while the other sneaked up to try to find the leveret hidden in the grass. So the hare left her first persecutor to attack the second and the battle swung from one to the other as the hare tried to defend in two directions.

The drama went on for hour after hour for two days and I can't help thinking that the crows had all the leverets but one. Why the hare didn't take them into thicker cover I shall never know, but at last I could stand the persecution no longer. So I fetched the rifle and turned the tide of battle.

Without that intervention, the odds against that young hare surviving would have been very long indeed.

# 16. Crises in front of the television camera

Things which are fun to look forward to, and even more fun to look back on, are often hell at the time. I find with television that nothing ever seems to go right. But every goose that goes in at one end of the camera might come out as a swan on the screen.

Some time ago I was invited to take part in a *Look Stranger* television film based on the work I am doing in my wildlife reserve. It was a delightful idea – in prospect!

Filming at Goat Lodge, with the 'Look Stranger' film crew

So I spent a stimulating weekend showing Derek Trimby, the producer, the herons, the deer, the dogs, the Bagot goats, the pool, and every corner of the wood. We talked of my childhood days, poking about in Black Country swags for newts, and the life sentence I served in industry before breaking free to work for myself. Each thing we saw seemed to delight him more than the last and I became convinced that this was to be the film to end all films. There was so much visual material that we couldn't fail.

When we parted we were full of confidence, and agreed that the first sequence we would film would be when I gave Fred, my barn own, her liberty in June. As the film approached my confidence sagged. The film was to run for twenty-five minutes, which is a long time to fill without padding. Even if the birds and animals did do their stuff, they couldn't tell a story. Only I could do that. It slowly dawned on me that, although I couldn't make the thing a success, it would be all too easy for me to be the architect of its failure.

We kicked off with a double bonus. The week before I had decided to set Fred free, it became obvious that the roe deer was going to have her kid. She obliged two days before we were due to film and although I didn't know exactly where she had hidden her new-born kid, I was pretty sure it was somewhere in the triangle of woodland near the house.

When all was ready, I walked quietly over with Tick, my pointer, and within a minute or so, she had winded the kid and was standing statuesque, her forefoot poised, pointing at a clump of thick grass. Some television cameramen take twenty minutes to set up for a shot and, if this had happened, it would have been our first disaster. Tick wouldn't have held her point that long and, once she knew where the kid was, she would have gone straight back to it without the picturesque ritual of 'pointing'.

So our second bit of luck was to have Derek Johnson as cameraman. He spends most of his life filming news stories and gets his camera on target quicker than a cowboy can pull a gun.

Before we realised what was happening, Tick was 'in the can' and all I had to do was to part the grass at which she had been pointing. When they are very young, deer do not seek safety in flight, but rely instead on their marvellous camouflage. Crouched in the centre of the tussock at which Tick had been pointing, was a tiny spotted kid, no bigger than a rabbit. Derek leaned gently over and squirted off some more film. Within seconds, the delicate beauty of this new-born deer had joined Tick on the permanent record in his can.

Fred the barn owl was just as co-operative. We began in my study, where she spent the daytime, and she was as unselfconscious as if she'd been hatched under an arc light. She postured before the camera and went into close-up preening my bushy eyebrows with her lethal bill. When we set her free, she flew confidently back to the owl cote I had built for her, and then we had our first setback. As she alighted on the gable end of the roof, the swallows which nest in the garage spotted her and went into a spectacular dive-bombing attack at the precise moment the film ran out!

We took no more film until October, when we did a full week. One of the technical snags in filming animals is that it is often necessary to get the action repeated so that the camera can film the same shot from two different angles. This is so that a long piece of film can be cut as short as the producer wishes without it being obvious to the viewer. This is all right with people who can be instructed to repeat the same thing time after time, but it is often almost impossible with animals.

A deer, for example, may come fearlessly towards a strange man with a whirring camera but be quite terrified if it thinks he is trying to cut off its escape to safety. My fallow fawn was so co-operative that she bounded out of the wood to come freely up to me while the camera crew was about six feet behind me. She even stayed where she was for about five minutes while the camera was resited about eighty yards away to get a reverse angle shot to give the film a perfect ending as the lense zoomed out to shrink us into infinity.

We had our share of bad luck too! One crew turned up to film the herons. There was the producer, cameraman, assistant cameraman, sound engineer, lighting man and continuity girl. I made it crystal clear that herons were shy birds and that if such a gaggle of strangers hove in view there wouldn't be a bird in sight. So they brought a special hand-held camera so that only the cameraman and I need go anywhere near. As soon as he started to shoot, he discovered his battery was flat. By the time it was replaced, the herons had gone, and to add insult to injury, the battery on the other camera packed up too.

We spent ages trying to film the dogs jumping a five-barred gate. I had to send them over once so that everyone could see where to site the camera. They went over again to check if it could hold focus from take-off to landing. Mandy, the old lurcher, is a cunning old bitch who reckoned rehearsals a waste of energy. So when the time came to do the real thing, she had found an easier place and didn't go over the gate at all.

When we were filming in the house, I noticed a group of fallow deer coming out of the wood to feed in the ride in front of the window. If they had been tame instead of wild it would have been impossible to give the camera a better chance. When the rushes were developed, there were four scratches down the length of the film and it was unusable. When we got the chance to repeat the filming, it was pouring with rain and the deer were twice as far away.

We finished up with twelve days' filming to produce three and a half hours of film. And that had to be cut to twenty-five minutes. Before we started I knew the animals would be fine and that my friends, who share the work, were also going to share the film. But I was quite right about it being hell at the time.

# Summer

# 17. Should a farmer picnic on your front lawn?

People who know nothing about the country code must be illiterate. We are continually subjected to such a barrage of pleas and advice that even the most dedicated conservationists have begun to hiccup with mental indigestion. I am very conscious of this because I was painting the countryside in words designed to deter people from despoiling it long before the 'code' was so much as a twinkle in someone's eye. And with luck my typewriter will still be bashing it out when all the fanfares have subsided.

This seems a good time to strike a balance by looking at the other side of the penny. Not so much at what we are trying to conserve, as why and at whose expense. Our village street, for example, has been designated a Conservation Area. That means that the people who own the houses cannot alter their external appearance without special planning permission. Even small traders, anxious to compete by modern selling techniques, cannot jazz up their shop fronts. The idea is that visitors shall see a village as picturesque in the future as it was in the past. The fact that the cottages are as 'dampe' as they are 'olde worlde' matters only to those who live in them.

The modern fashion of believing that because things are old they are good can stretch to ridiculous lengths. People who spend seven nights a week in isolated cottages can be denied television as their only entertainment because strangers who venture from their urban jungle only in fair weather think it would spoil their view if a television mast were stuck on a convenient hill. And it is easy to object to electric pylons stitching across the countryside's fair face if the alternative is paraffin lamps for somebody else.

Conservation should be inseparable from compromise. A century ago it was fashionable to be a collector and to exhibit folios of pressed flowers or cabinets of birds' eggs or butterflies crucified on pins. The rarer they were, the greater their status value so that some species were collected to the point of extinction. The pendulum now has swung the other way. I soon grew out of the collecting mania, but while it lasted it

# Please don't be a . . . . .

Lavinia Litterlout

Bernard Blazer

Ferocious Fido

Relentless Richard

Poisonous Percy

Reckless Ringo

Dreamy Desmond

Heedless Henry

Polly Plantpuller

## Respect the life of the countryside

Good manners are essential in the country

fired me with a love of country things which has never been quenched. If I'd never stolen a bird's egg I might never have been interested.

It is so important to rouse the enthusiasm of the coming generation that a few eggs lost in the process may spell salvation for thousands to come. It is just as stupid to be a doctrinaire crank. Being dedicated to stopping everyone doing what you don't happen to agree with is as stupid as it is to maintain that the countryside and everything in it is there to be enjoyed as a right by all.

I like the story of the farmer who caught a gaggle of picknickers in the middle of his hay and took their names and addresses. Next weekend he motored to their house, drove his Land Rover across their rosebed and set up his picnic table in the middle of their lawn. They saw his point about the hay.

The privilege of wandering in the country carries responsibilities with it. Many are trying to wrest a living from ungenerous land and all are potential victims of thoughtless behaviour or deliberate vandalism. Even a tiny minority of unthinking visitors can cause intense irritation and material damage. They can push the natives to a homicidal mental state. Yet fools who let their dogs chase stock grow cross when they are shot.

Most public footpaths were not made for amusement of the masses but to allow neighbours to take short cuts to work. Now that farm methods have changed and demand large fields to allow expensive machinery to pay its way, it would seem sensible at least to divert footpaths round their boundaries. Yet gangs of Heedless Henrys, who would yowl their their heads off if a stranger wandered into their garden, insist on tramping through fields of corn on other people's land just for their amusement.

Those who enjoy shooting game or fishing are usually prepared to pay for their sport by renting the rights over the land or water where they want to go. As a naturalist, I believe that I and others like me should be equally prepared to put our hands in our pockets. When president of a county nature conservation trust, I found that there are indeed a large number of people who will. They raised the money to buy an important wood which would otherwise have fallen to the woodman's axe.

Having got a bird sanctuary, I think we owe responsibility to the birds as well as the birdwatchers. I do not think it is our right to disturb their nests for photographs, or net them for ringing, or crowd them out of their security by sheer human pressure. Although nobody is keener on conservation than I am, I should like to believe that among the things to be conserved are the basic rights, not only of wildlife but of those who own the land where it survives.

# 18. Summer signs

An old wives' tale insists that you can tell good summers and bad in advance by where the moorhens nest. "If they build well up in the bank," it says, "that's a sign of floodwater and a lot of rain. Lower to the water's edge is a sign of dry weather." The soothsayer established her credential for expounding such country lore by telling me that her dear old dad killed thousands of foxes and badgers. "The ruddy foxes are a real pest," she said. "I should know because my dad was a head gamekeeper in Hertfordshire, and I have a brother in Shropshire who loves the job. He killed forty-two in one day and has only one eye."

Whatever your views about killing 'thousands' of foxes and badgers, there is no argument that those capable of such feats are likely to have forgotten more about elementary country things than most of us will ever know. I always respect the opinions of such people because I have learned from experience that apparently far-fetched snippets of folklore are often near the truth. If my informant is right, the moorhens must have built on stilts because flaming June gurgled itself into obscurity with enough storm water to flush the streams and overflow the pools.

There are lots of similar scraps of folklore that make apparent nonsense. "If rooks build high it will be a good summer. If they put their nests down on firmer branches we are in for storm and hurricane." The fact is that most rookeries are in about the same place in the trees every year, whatever the weather. It is not until hurricanes actually blow the nests out of the exposed places that the survivors can be seen where, with hindsight, it would have been more prudent for the victims to have built as well.

"If there are lots of holly and hawthorn berries, it will be a hard winter" could probably be written more accurately as "lots of berries are an indication that it was a good spring when the fruit was setting".

The weathermen on the radio seem incapable of accurate forecasts a single day ahead, despite all their complicated contranklements. Perhaps they would do better to go moorhen nesting in spring. For my part, I never stick my neck out. I enjoy most sorts of weather except bitter east winds and have lived long enough to know that whatever traditions pretend, it is rarely white at Christmas and rarely flames in June. Depression over the Atlantic and new-fangled pollen counts mean less to me than the first snowdrop at the turn of the year, or blackberries and mushrooms in autumn.

Summer never seems summer without the affectionate crooning of turtle doves and I have been far more worried about their scarcity than about the inhospitable wet weather that may have caused it. Turtle doves look rather like collared doves which have saddled us with their wretched population explosion. I have had as many as thirty feeding on my bird table and even this was only a quarter of the flock that gorged at my expense all winter on corn I put out for the wild duck. It isn't their greed that wears out their welcome or the fact that they came uninvited or that they have such monotonous voices. I dislike them because they are such disagreeable little birds that they tend to keep gentler birds out. They were once kept in cages as domestic turtle doves but they are larger than the delightful birds which visit us in summer and they have a distinctive black collar round the back of their necks.

Real turtle doves have blue-grey on their crowns and the napes of their necks, with chestnut bellies and spotted mantles. But it is the voice of the turtle dove that spells summer to me. It is a most soothing and seductive croon which permeates the whole countryside as subtly as the hot air eddies of mirages on our rare scorching days.

This year the first turtle doves delighted us but departed again almost at once. Perhaps they were driven off by their aggressive cousins, the collared doves which stayed all winter when they migrated, or they may have retreated from one cold spot to the next, like holiday-makers dodging the dragons who keep inhospitable digs. A week or so ago another pair of turtle doves came and settled in the corner of the wood on the far side of the pool and their musical crooning was the first sound to drift through the open bedroom window at dawn.

The weather was still wet and the wind still bitter enough to gripe my guts with colic – but for me summer had come at last. The sappy green grass forgot the deluge and stiffened from aquatic mush to virile seedheads which suited my young pheasants far better than hard-boiled egg and chick crumbs. The wind dropped enough at sunset to let sweet honeysuckle scent the evening air, luring the hawkmoths from shelter, and duck flighted on and off the pool, weaving patterns on the still surface.

Then I got a bonus. A real summer bonus. One of our tame roe deer came out on the paddock with her month-old kid. She had hidden it till then for it was still no bigger than a hare but with legs so long and spindly that they seemed too fragile and delicate to support even such a sprite in safety. I watched, entranced, through powerful field glasses which brought it almost near enough to stroke. My concentration was such that I hadn't noticed an old vixen come out on the ride with a cub, but when I looked up, she was right in the open. Tame roe deer and wild foxes in view at the same instant, with the lullaby of turtle doves as mood-music! Whatever the weathermen say, there will never be a more summery night for me.

# 19. One of nature's mysteries

By the beginning of May, the faintest softening of outline hinted that our young roe deer had indulged in more than a mild flirtation last summer. The kid she had last year is now a handsome young buck with his first pair of antlers as sharp and pointed as a puppy's milk teeth. Each year, as he grows older, his new pair of antlers will improve until he passes his prime and they will begin to deteriorate again. He was born on May 13 last year, but his mother did not drop her kid this time until May 26.

When roe kids are born, they are tiny sprites about as big as rabbits. The colour of their coats is bright foxy-red and it is spotted with a startling white pattern which is most conspicuous – when you see it. But this pattern only stands out from its background when you *do* spot

**The young fawn hidden in the reed bed**

it. Until then, it breaks up the outline of the kid and it is easy to pass within arm's reach thinking that it is a bunch of whitening leaves left by the wind among the winter withered grass.

This year has been an exceptionally late season. The lush russet bracken bed, which was the doe's accouchement pad last year, was only an arid mattress of dried waste, with scarcely a green frond for privacy or shelter. So, it wasn't born till a fortnight later when there was more cover to conceal it. I couldn't help wondering if this was accidental or if the old doe really did have any control over the time she gave birth.

The theory is not as far fetched as it may seem. Roe deer are already known to have at least one odd facet in their pregnancy known as delayed implantation. Although they mate in July, the embryo does not even begin to develop until December, and the young are born the next May. Some scientists believe that Nature arranges for roe deer to mate in prime conditions of summer feed, but does not tax the mother's strength by carrying young in an advanced state of development till the worst of the winter is past. Badgers and seals show the same phenomenon, but even the cleverest scientists have to admit that it is one of the wonders of Nature which still baffles them.

When our doe eventually did have her kid, the bracken was still not mature enough for cover, so she had it in a thick reed bed by the pool. The tiny kid was so delicate and its legs so slender that it could only move about in these reeds in a series of clumsy lurches. A child of five, if his eyes had been sharp enough to penetrate its camouflage, could easily have caught it.

The mother only went near it every few hours, when she uttered a series of high-pitched bleats. The kid accepted this invitation at once, crept from the privacy of its couch and staggered over to suckle from the doe. While it was feeding, she groomed and cleaned and licked it, clearing up any droppings that were left so that there would be no tell-tale scent to attract predators which might eat the kid. When she had fed it, she sent it back to lie quiet in the nest or form, till she visited it again.

I watched the whole procedure through powerful glasses several times but have never been able to discover how she persuaded it to return to its hiding place. It is easy to see how a mother can call a hungry youngster to her, yet to make it go away from her protection and hide by itself implies some sort of animal language.

I have heard naturalists say, in such cases, that mothers take their young right to the spot they have selected for them to hide and then somehow force them to lie there. This would taint the spot with the scent of the mother as well as the kid, and it certainly didn't happen when I was watching. But although I watched the whole performance most carefully, I am still no wiser now as to how she persuaded that kid to do its party trick than if they had belonged to the Magic Circle.

# 20. Welcome squatters

We usually have a wonderful crop of swallows. The pair in the garage are now feeding their third lot of young and they reared a family of four fledglings in each of the earlier broods. The other pair have reared six in the shed, which was the cottage earth closet before we installed modern sanitation. The total of these two pairs is already fourteen and there is a fair chance that the last four may mature in time to emigrate successfully to sunny Africa.

This is a good indication that conditions here are normally almost ideal. The swarms of flies, which make the air in the wood vibrate with their humming, must provide an inexhaustible supply of food. The mud at the edge of the pool is of the right consistency for them to build their nest with a couple of days' labour, and the old birds are in such perfect condition that the fertility of their eggs was excellent.

That makes it seem all the more strange that our house martins have done worse than in any season since we came. They are so like swallows that many people can't tell them apart. House martins have white underparts and their forked tails look webbed compared with the streamer tails of swallows. Swallows have lovely chestnut foreheads and chins and throats, but I find the easiest way to tell them is when they are flying directly away. Then the white rumps of house martins make them look like butterflies flitting about.

Besides being so similar in appearance, swallows and martins like similar conditions. Both feed on the wing by catching flying insects. Both drink at full speed on the wing by scooping up water as old-fashioned steam trains did from a trough between the lines. They both make their nests basically of mud. Swallows fashion an open saucer, but martins cement their nest to the walls and overhanging eaves, leaving a hole only large enough for their entrance.   So it seems logical that if the swallows do well, the house martins should be just as happy. Yet when we came to the cottage six years ago, there were swallows nesting in the pigsty, but never a house martin in sight. I was disappointed about this because I am equally fond of both. Oddly enough, so was my father though he was never as interested in general natural history as I am. I remember that when he built a house in Bloxwich he insisted on overhanging, plastered eaves specially designed to attract the house martins to nest. They never obliged him and the whole time he was there, from 1924 until he retired a few years ago, his eaves were as bare of nests as the day they were built.

By the time we came to Goat Lodge, ornithologists had discovered that house martins will nest as freely in properly designed artificial nests as blue tits will in hollow logs. Having a practical nature, I bought one nest as a model and made several others to the same pattern which I installed under the eaves. I then discovered that half coconut shells, with the correct sized holes, are quite satisfactory.

The first year, one pair took to one of these artificial nests and two more pairs built conventional mud nests of their own. After that, word went round that ours was an attractive building site. The little colony increased to seven pairs by which time we could hardly see out of one bedroom window for the mess they made. It was a small price to pay for perhaps forty or fifty young martins, and this year we looked forward to such clouds of swallows and martins hawking flies over the paddock that hardly an insect would survive to penetrate the defences of the house.

It turned out to be a vain hope. Nothing in Nature goes according to plan. The swallows turned up at the beginning of the season and so did a couple of pairs of house martins. The swallow nesting sites inside the buildings are undisturbed, but since last year the honeysuckle on the gable end has grown so lush that it has plastered the whole wall with sweetly scented flowers. House martins like flies but not flowers which are so dense that they give foothold for sparrows; so the martins did not even try to nest there.

I normally knock out all martin nests at the end of each season because if I leave them the sparrows enlarge the holes, roost in them all winter, and nest in them in spring. House martins then find it impossible to evict them when they return, and seek an alternative site. It is far better to let them build new nests for themselves, which they can usually defend against all-comers.

Even so, a couple of martins built nests under the dormer windows, but the sparrow colony was so strong that they gave up the struggle and went away, leaving a cocky pair of victorious sparrows in possession of their new nests. Their triumph was short lived. I had no scruples about dealing with these. But even when I had removed them the martins were nowhere to be seen, and we thought we were back where we began. It was another example of the truth that there is no such thing as the balance of Nature, and that if things are left strictly to themselves, the strong nearly always flourish at the expense of the weak.

Ten days ago, our management of the sparrows paid dividends. Waking at first light, I was delighted to see a pair of house martins refurbishing one of the nests the sparrows had stolen. Within twenty-four hours, it was nearly complete. Now they are incubating a clutch of eggs there, even though I fear it is a bit late in the season to rear young strong enough to survive the tough migration flight to Africa. But the minor success in management has encouraged me to try more vigorously next year to re-establish a thriving colony. The old honeysuckle is set for a severe bashing, and any sparrows rash enough to show their beaks will be encouraged to move on to hosts more hospitable than me.

I shall erect a new set of artificial nests with tailor-made front doors, and show in every way that I can that, however much mess the swallows and martins may make, no guests who come to our house are more welcome.

# 21. My garden for a deer

I am often asked for advice about the conflicting interests of the countryside. Last week it was the deer on Cannock Chase which have always been catalysts of controversy. Some of them had not had the manners to wait for an invitation to dine on the roses in surrounding gardens – and the gardeners were very cross indeed. One of the protestors even wanted an enclosure erected in the middle of the Chase and all the deer confined there. The slickest cowboys would find King Canute's task of turning the tide kid's stuff compared to such a round-up.

As with so many conflicting interests in the countryside, there is no

A fallow deer

easy answer. Deer lovers, especially those who don't live near deer, say
that the gardeners should move to a town where blackfly and blight are
the roses' only enemies. With luck, there might be enough smoke in the
air to stifle the blight. Dedicated gardeners might say shoot all the deer
and turn them into venison. The halfway house of catching them, and
confining them in miniature Whipsnades, is equally impractical.

Nor is it any better to take the law into one's own hands. I have heard
that infuriated gardeners have shot six deer for raiding gardens within
the last few weeks. I don't know if this is an exaggeration but it is certainly true that at least two deer have been blinded by shotguns. They
would have died a lingering and painful death but for the vigilance of
Forestry officials who followed them up and put them out of their
misery.

I hope that the culprits will be traced and prosecuted and that public
opinion will discourage such people who take the law into their own
hands. In any case, such action is illegal because this is the close season
for fallow deer. The does are suckling their young and if they are killed
now, their fawns are left to starve. It is only legal to shoot them out of
season by special licence, which is granted only in cases of exceptional
damage. It is also illegal to shoot deer at any time with shot guns that
are not firing special cartridges designed for deer because of the high
risk of leaving them wounded to die.

The storm about deer robbing the roses is still whizzing round its
teacup. We live by a wood where fallow deer roam. Nobody is a keener
gardener than my wife and few people enjoy watching wildlife more
than I do, so we can see the problem from both sides. Our solution has
been to keep the vulnerable part of the garden as small as possible. This
has the enormous advantage that my wife can cope, and I can admire
her work in comfort with an easy conscience. It also means that, for the
price of a few rose bushes, we have been able to fence the garden safe
from deer, and plant a hedge to hide the fence inside the netting. She
gets her roses and I feed the wild deer with maize, so that they delight us
both by coming close to the house, on the site where we left the wood
instead of making a garden.

We have avoided living in a town because we prefer seclusion and
privacy to urban amenities. Trudging through deep snow or mud

seems to us a small price to pay. By the same token, people should not settle where deer are a priceless amenity if they object to taking the trouble to safeguard a few flowers which would grow as well in a back street.

The impossibility of pleasing everyone is a growing problem in the countryside. More and more people have leisure and easy transport to take them to secluded places. There are more people snarling over every sheet of water than there are jackals round a lion's kill. Some want to watch wild birds under natural conditions and to be left in peace. Others want to charge round on water skis behind thundering power boats. Some want to fish, some to shoot the duck the bird-watchers are photographing, and others only want to play with sailing boats, or to paint idyllic scenes.

Every village is growing, swollen by commuters who bring from their towns demands for street lamps where country lads have always done their courting in decent privacy. Hillsides are topped with pylons and television masts, bringing convenience to wild places but spoiling the view.

Some are delighted, others furious. You can't please them all; even the most reasonable compromise demands considerable sacrifice. The sensible thing is not to set up home where it is perfectly obvious that the natural character of the place is incompatible with yours. Don't live by a hay field if you suffer from hay fever, or in a town if you are claustrophobic. If roses, which thrive anywhere, are the light of your eyes, don't go where you will annoy the neighbours by shooting the deer. It is easier to grow your roses in an inaccessible window box. And you will be far less unpopular with your country-loving neighbours.

# 22. Naturalists' primer

There are various ways of becoming a good naturalist. The fashionable one at the moment is to graduate from being an eager beaver in the rural studies class at the local primary school to the dizzy heights of Doctor of Philosophy. This is usually conferred on those who write a learned thesis after taking a biology degree at university. I mention it because it is the way I would have least confidence in recommending. Society has gone so education-mad that it is in danger of ignoring the primitive laws of supply and demand.

Our mass production academic machine is churning out more highly qualified boffins than there are jobs for them to fill. I know several bachelors of science and doctors of philosophy who have been out of work for months.

An alternative, but more difficult way is to arrange to be born into the family of a country parson. It is a profession that benefits from meditation about the wonders of nature. *The Natural History of Selborne* by the Rev. Gilbert White was published in 1788 and has been a best-seller ever since.

Some of the most knowledgeable of my friends have been poachers or gamekeepers who have little in common with vicars. The success of either depends on acute observation and the ability to wait patiently and move silently. Countless hours alone in quiet places can fill a deeper and more original pool of knowledge than a bagful of books mugged up in the local library.

Yet even those practical men are sometimes taken for a ride. One morning, when I was about twelve, I was wandering quietly down a farm track with one of the cleverest poachers it has been my privilege to meet. The sun was already up and, since we had no right to be there, we were hugging the shadow of hedges and trees and patches of dead ground. The slightest wave of Jimmy's hand was all the signal I needed to freeze in my tracks, but when I followed the direction of his eyes I realised that nobody had spotted us.

A hare was squatting motionless between the heel of a five-bar gate and the post six inches away. My companion stooped stealthily and scooped up a great pebble – 'bibble' he called it – as big as his fist. With the unerring aim of a wicketkeeper exploding the bails, he slung his bibble slap into the ribs of the hare. No living creature could have survived such a thump, but it caused his victim no discomfort. When we picked her up, it was all too obvious that she had lain dead and rigid between the gate and its post for far too long to be healthy. I've often wondered since if someone had put that dead hare there as a practical joke or if it was her last refuge when she was hunted by a stoat.

It is a traditional trick to play in the country on trigger-happy marksmen who ignore the sportsmen's code of giving their quarry a sporting chance. A dead hare or pheasant is set-up with all the skill of a taxidermist where there will be the temptation to take a pot shot at it without giving it chance to get up and run or fly away. Even the thickest skinned shooter feels stupid when he discovers that he's been caught falling for such a ploy.

One of my party tricks is to persuade hares to come towards me instead of taking flight. It works best in spring when they have young scattered around in separate forms. Their mother, the old doe, is constantly on the look-out for danger and will sometimes attack stoats and rats and crows that are threatening her leverets. Any aggressor less than her own size is most unwise to risk a knock-out kick from her powerful back legs.

It is not difficult to suck air through moistened lips to make a noise like the high-pitched squeal of a young rabbit or leveret in distress. The sound has a remarkable effect on adult hares and stoats and foxes. They are easily convinced that it is some vulnerable young creature. So the hares come up to defend it while the predators stalk round in the hopes of an easy meal.

Keepers use the sound to bring foxes and stoats along the last steps to the gibbet. Poachers call hares within range of silent catapults and gipsies call them into the open to give their lurchers a run. It is an accomplishment that impresses observers quite out of proportion to the skill it involves, and otherwise knowledgeable people are obviously surprised by those who can 'call wild animals to them'.

My friend Stanley Porter spent most of his leisure hours sitting in a hide by day, taking photographs of birds. So far as I can judge from his enormous output, he must have spent most of his nights developing and printing the pictures he took. When he had spent countless unsuccessful hours waiting for a hare to come lolloping along within range of his telephoto lens, I decided to do something about it. He was highly respectable, not addicted to poachers' tricks, so I taught him to 'squeak them up'.

If you should decide to try it for yourself, there is just one more poachers' trick you should know. Be certain to have ready a likely story for your presence first. A keeper catching you at it may need some convincing that your reason for calling up his game is incontestably innocent.

# 23. Strawberry scoffers

Although I like my food, I make no pretence of being a connoisseur of continental concoctions. Those who disguise their meat with garlic are probably trying to fob me off with the flesh of horse or ancient cows long past their prime. I suspect all dishes messed about with such exotic sauces that only the chef knows how they started life. Frogs or snails or squid may be good enough for the natives, but I want none of them.

If I could choose my favourite meal, I would start with roast duckling with young green peas and new potatoes. All I should want after that would be fresh strawberries and cream.

To gratify this whim, while I reared a dozen Aylesbury ducklings, my wife lavished her loving care on the strawberry bed. The ducks were

A short-tailed field vole having a quiet nibble

clothed in down when they hatched and their first covering of snow white feathers was just complete at ten weeks old. That would have been the time to kill them – if they were grown for profit. The largest would have weighed about seven pounds and have been superbly tender. Since the young feathers were just complete, they would have been easy to pluck.

I rear my ducklings not for my profit, but my pleasure. So I let them grow on for another few weeks, by which time their adult crop of feathers was complete. It would have been almost impossible to have plucked them in the intervening weeks because immature quills would have stuck out all over them as intractable as the stubble on an old tramp's chin.

At fourteen weeks, our biggest drakes were just ten pounds and I admit that I had fed them for a whole month to gain those extra three pounds. Not commercially viable perhaps, but what superb ducks they were. More mature; their flesh was firmer yet still young enough to be tender, simply roasted, without any of the disguises beloved by foreigners.

My wife had less luck with the tag-end of the feast. She caressed the strawberry plants with her green fingers, spoiled them with fragrant rotted compost from the cow sheds, and cosseted them with a mattress of clean straw. All went well at the start. The plants were robust and full of promise. They flowered lavishly and the young fruits set with wanton generosity.

Then she suddenly noticed piles of unripe fruit gathered and stored under the shadiest leaves in the strawberry bed. Rabbits were currently top of her hate-list because they were raiding her flower beds, but I pointed out that, whatever their faults, the miserly hoarding of food for mythical rainy days was not one of them. The alibi was completed by the fact that she grows her strawberries and raspberries in a fruit cage of wire netting so fine that even the sparrows cannot breach her defences.

The culprits therefore must have been smaller than birds and she remembered seeing several frogs there. I knew that they too were innocent, though they did lead me off on a false trail. Frogs feed on slugs and slugs like fruit. But they do not hoard it for the future.

It was the badgers which eventually put me on the scent. At this time of year, I usually find large spherical holes scooped out in the ground where badgers have dug out wasp nests for the grubs. I haven't found one yet, nor have I seen more than a score of wasps, so that I hope the cold wet weeks earlier on killed off most of the queens. But I have found scores of holes where the badgers have dug out the nest of short-tailed voles. Instead of being up to the size of a football, as a wasp nest would be, these holes would fit a tennis ball and there is usually a tell-tale litter of chewed grasses that the victims carried in for their nests. Badgers can't get into the fruit cage, neither can owls nor hawks which like voles to eat as much as I like strawberries.

So the voles have found sanctuary where they can feast with impunity on the luscious fruit my wife has grown. I proved the point by catching five the first day I put my traps between the rows of plants. We haven't suffered before because there have been relatively few voles and the damage they have done has been insignificant. This year, as the nests dug out by the badgers confirm, there has been such a plague of voles that they have scoffed practically all our strawberries.

They are a species which are unusually prone to dramatic fluctuations. Conditions must have suited them and they have been feather-bedded by climate and food supply so that their teeming numbers have exploded.

But doom, in the shape of owls or hawks or weasels or disease, will surely catch up with them so that next year, I hope, we shall be able to grow masses of strawberries which will ripen unmolested. Or they will if it isn't the year when slugs and snails proliferate, or the weather is so wet that it rots the fruit, or so dry that the berries shrivel. Nature is unbeatable and I am glad that she is. Whenever one species is too successful, she devises something to cut it down to size again.

Perhaps our strawberries will do fine after all next year, but foxes or stoats will kill the ducks. Our green peas will wither with blight, or there won't be any apples for the apple sauce. But such perfect food wouldn't be half as attractive if it was as easy to get as any pre-packed mush you can buy in a tin.

# 24. Owls improve the beef

It may not have occurred to you, but the superb flavour of English beef owes much to the humble German bumble bee. There are about twenty-five species of bumble bees, ranging from an inch or so long to less than a quarter that size. The relationship between these wild bees and your Sunday lunch is not as distant as you might think.

Some years ago, observant Germans noticed that crops of red clover were heavier near to villages than in the open countryside, far from human habitation. This was very important in districts where the production of red clover seed was an important local industry, so scientists set out to discover any factors which affected the fertility of the crop for better or for worse.

It had long been realised that red clover was difficult for many insects to fertilise by carrying pollen from one flower to another, because the flower trumpets are so deep and narrow. Only insects with tongues long enough and flexible enough to probe for nectar to the base of the trumpets of the flowers could carry away the pollen to breathe life into the seeds of the next generation. Bumble bees happen to be admirably suited to this task because their tongues are so abnormally long that they find the tortuous tunnels of red clover flowers as simple to negotiate as orchids for a humming bird.

As a result, wherever bumble bees thrived, red clover was exceptionally prolific. At first sight, this appeared to have no connection with the proximity of the nearest village, for why should bumble bees thrive if they shared their estate with a colony of Common Man?

The scientists started to unravel the mystery by making a study of the habits of bumble bees. They do not live in hives or hollow trees, like domestic bees or bees gone wild. When the queen comes out of hibernation in spring, for she is the only member of the colony to survive the winter, she searches hedges and uncultivated ground for a suitable hole in which to make her nest and lay her eggs as the foundation for her hive. This hole will be about $3/_4$in. in diameter and will usually penetrate underground for three to five inches. The end of the tunnel will bell out into a cavity about as large as a tennis ball. This cavity will be filled with a beautifully soft bed of dried grass, chewed to short lengths which will give all the luxury of a fine down pillow.

The main creatures which build such desirable accommodation are fieldmice and voles – and they could be persuaded to allow a stinging bumble bee to share their homes only over their dead bodies. Over their dead bodies is the key to the mystery. There are more dead fieldmice and voles which leave homes with vacant possession near villages than in the open country. The reason is simply that village cats kill a higher percentage of their local wild mice than would die by the tooth of hunters in parts remote from man.

House hunting near villages is then easy. The abnormally high density of the bumble bee population near villages accounts for the more thorough pollination of red clover in these areas than in wilder places where bumble bees are scarcer. When the observant Germans tumbled to this fact, they set about finding a predator which would sort out the mice in remote places as efficiently as the cats near villages had done.

The obvious strong-arm men – or strong-wing birds – were owls. So the Germans took great care that nobody damaged an owl, and they erected scores of nesting boxes to encourage more owls to build where they wanted to grow their red clover. It is useless to get a bird to breed freely if there are no facilities for it to catch the prey to feed its young. There were plenty of succulent mice there all right, but it was difficult for the owls to get above them to see where to pounce in a featureless field.

So the methodical Germans put up T perches in rows down their clover fields. The owls accepted the invitation by leaving their nests and perching just where the Germans wanted them to, till they saw the telltale movements in the grass which told them where to pounce on a mouse. One swoop on muted wings accounted for that mouse and the next killed his mate, leaving a mouse nest vacant for the first bumble bee on tour in search of a nest.

All the mod. cons. of soft bedding, a one-way tunnel to control central heating and air humidity were available for the bumble bees. Such estates of fine houses with an easy living on the doorstep attracted a far higher density of bumble bees than would have settled naturally.

Because their livelihood happened to depend on the nectar of red clover flowers, they soon paid their rent by supplying an unusually high crop of pedigree clover seeds.

From these seeds grew the lush grazing to feed English cattle which flourished in our English climate to produce the sweetest beef this side of paradise. Its superb flavour owes much to the bumble bees which fertilised the clover which fed the bullocks which grew the beef. Which brings me back to where I started.

# 25. Road victim

Down in the rushes at the edge of our pool an old moorhen had been sitting on her nest of eggs for more than a fortnight. The incubation period is about three weeks. Although they are such common birds, I enjoy watching moorhens as much as if they were exotic rarities. Flashier kingfishers may look more impressive as they streak across the water, but when they come to rest they look out of proportion with too much head and beak for their puny under-sized bodies. It is only the trajectory of their flight that diverts attention to their gleaming colours.

The reverse is true of moorhens. Their flight is clumsy and weak, often so near the water that their barge-sized feet patter the surface into grey droplets. The first impression is that they are dull and dowdy. A

**Releasing the Great Crested Grebe when it had recovered from its injuries**

second glance reveals that they are far from slatterns. Their plumage is shot with subtle shades of greens and olives. The bill is as bright as good accessories should be for garments of restraint. It has a yellow tip which shades to brilliant red as it runs up to eye level. The tail coverts flaunt a white patch, and a slim white line running along the flank adds a final touch of elegance.

I was looking forward to seeing the chicks, not so much because moorhens are so easy on the eye as that they are such exemplary mothers. The way they collect tiny morsels of food and offer them to each chick in turn is an object lesson in unselfish devotion.

Such dedication might threaten a population explosion among moorhens if it was not that they have so many enemies. Foxes love them and crows devour their eggs and young. Other moorhens fight them, and coots and wild duck drown their chicks, presumably because they might grow up to compete with them for food. Boys with catapults and men with guns add to their perils, but our moorhen suffered tragedy at the hand of Fate not Man.

I was roused from sleep by rain bucketing down with the ferocity of a tropical storm. By evening, the level of the pool had risen six inches and the following morning I had serious qualms that the pressure of water would burst the banks. From the moorhen's point of view, it might have been a good thing if it had. But as things turned out, the level continued to rise, 'drowning' the nest and chilling the eggs so that the chicks didn't live to see the light of day.

It was not the only catastrophe. As I walked round the wood, I found waterlogged pheasant nests deserted so that their contents had been raided by crows. How many casualties remained hidden by the undergrowth is anybody's guess.

It highlighted the ease of taking for granted storm and drought, and deep snow and failed harvests. Such hazards must force all kinds of creature to cope with conditions for which they were never fitted – or perish. Sustained frosts starve birds like herons and kingfishers because their beaks were not designed as ice-breakers. Cold late springs delay the hatch of insects that are vital for young insectivorous birds. And when leaves are late developing, there is no cover for protection from predators.

Our moorhen's nest, which had survived intact within yards of the badger sett, illustrated the fact that badgers wreak less havoc than a few hours of exceptionally heavy rain.

By coincidence, on the same night, I came across a bird in trouble which would have found it simple to cope with the problem that had spelt doom for our moorhen. I was coming home late across the road which divides the two halves of Blithfield Reservoir when my headlights picked out a great crested grebe, dazed and helpless, in the middle of the road. I could scarcely believe my eyes because these grebes are not common on land and I had only seen them swimming or diving at the edge of the reeds in large lakes. I supposed that this one had been flying across the road and had collided with a car, so I scooped it up and took it home in the hope that I could heal it. It promptly speared my hand with its dagger of a beak to teach me to be gentle.

Great crested grebes are diving birds, created by Nature to catch fish in fair chase under water. Their legs are set so far back that they act like propellors on a power boat. And though they can stand on land, they cannot easily run fast enough to get airborne. So the bird on the road would almost certainly have been killed by a passing car if I had not rescued it.

The reason that a crested grebe's nest would have escaped the fate of my moorhen is quite simple. They are such specialised aquatic birds that water is more natural to them than land and they even build their nests on floating mats of vegetation. So when the water in their lakes ebbs and flows, rising or falling, the nest is a floating island, always safe from harm.

I had half-expected my injured bird to be dead next morning, so was delighted to find him alive, and anxious to jag me with his beak again. I gave him a thorough examination but could find no injuries, so I took him down to the edge of our pool and set him free. He waddled clumsily on the bank for a second but was utterly transformed the moment he touched the water. He zoomed to the centre of the pool, as effortlessly as a torpedo, and preened himself to cleanse the defilement left by human hands. Then he aquaplaned across the surface until he was going fast enough to get airborne, then circled once and set course for the Reservoir a couple of miles away.

I hope he found his mate floating on her nest safe from the worst our watery weather could chuck down.

# 26. What is the score for a bull?

Mathematics was high on my list of hates at school but, if logic could not jerk me out of my inertia, I found a phenomenon which sparked my acceleration till my feet twinkled faster than light.

I was about ten at the time and had been taken by my parents for a holiday on a farm near Burton Bradstock in Dorset. It was a large mixed farm so I can't imagine why I was expected to show enthusiasm for paddling in the surf or cricket on the sands. Although it was less than a mile from the beach, I never even saw the sea for the simple reason that I preferred messing about on the farm.

I watered the horses, and fed the pigs, and collected the eggs, but my most vivid recollection is of the Hereford bull. He was a very large bull indeed, a truly gigantic bull, but simple observations should have con-

Edward Froggatt and his new mammoth Galloway bull

vinced me that his size was matched by his docility. He had about forty cows grazing with him in a field half a mile or so from the house and he came quietly with them when they were driven up the lane to be milked. He returned equally sedately when their distended udders had been emptied into pails. This in itself was a fair measure of his tractability but to hammer the point home, the farmer's young son perched on his back as cheeky as the monkey on a barrel organ.

This lad soon discovered that I was a bit green so he set about convincing me that the old bull was savage with everyone but him. I had been brought up to beware of bulls so, despite the evidence of my own eyes, I believed him. When a newly-calved cow broke from the herd and galloped bellowing towards the cowshed where her calf was tethered, my young farmer friend roared, "Look out. The bull!"

I didn't stop to see if he was spoofing and it would have taken a wizard with a slide rule to calculate my velocity. Even in those days, I was built more for comfort than for speed, but the sound of snorts and thundering hooves elevated me to Olympic class. The five-barred gate to the fold yard loomed up higher than a church steeple but I never seemed to touch the top. I cleared it in a parabola which would have delighted my maths master – and landed up to my armpits in the muck pit. My only consolation was the hiding the farmer's son collected because his mother blamed him for the trail of defilement I left up to the bathroom.

I was reminded of the incident the other day when a new bull arrived on the farm next door. He is a pedigree Galloway of proportions as prodigious as the Hereford of my childhood. And he is as soft as a mop, at any rate with humans.

Living in the country, it is wise to know not only where bulls are kept, but which bulls are known to be savage, so as soon as I saw him I asked how his temper was. My neighbour Edward Froggatt and his bull replied with a display of mutual affection, for the great animal stood motionless to have the top of his head scratched. He obviously revelled in such attention and wore an expression of soppy bliss as if an evil thought had never crossed his mind.

This in itself was deceptive. The reason for his sojourn near us turned out to be that he had proved almost impossible to contain on the farm where he belonged a couple of miles away. It was not that he had chivvied his owner. He only flew into uncontrollable rages at the sight of the other bull which shared his herd. Splitting up a battle between two such combatants does nothing for one's prospects of ripe old age, so it was decided to put the width of Blithfield reservoir between them.

Having seen the demonstrations of scratching his pate, I am no longer worried about meeting him should he get out. On the whole, beef breeds are fairly tractable and the largest Hereford and Angus and Galloway bulls are less dangerous than Jerseys or other beasts produced for milk. A year or so ago, a Friesian bull was monarch of the cows in the fields along our lane and he made quite an impact on the district. As soon as he caught sight of a stranger, he showed the whites of his eyes and snorted. Then he began to rumble in his belly a˜ he pawed the ground to hollow out a mark to launch himself into a charge. To add conviction, he dug first one horn and then the other into the turf, sending the clods sailing through the air as high as bottles at a football match. It was an effective weapon of psychological warfare, designed to demoralise opponents before battle was joined. Few stopped to see the whole ritual because only the stupid hung around until he charged.

I was most sorry for Mabel, our postwoman. Despite the cost of postage, a mail van is a luxury which has not yet reached our neck of the backwoods. Our post is peddled round on a push bike as I imagine it was at the turn of the century when bicycles were as modern as tomorrow and the price of sending a letter was an 'old' – or proper – penny. The round is thirteen miles or so over rough lanes in all weathers so, not surprisingly, the post doesn't arrive very early. We are lucky to see it before eleven or half past in the morning.

When the Friesian bull saw the letters arriving, he trundled along the other side of the hedge looking for a gap to break through. This wouldn't have mattered with a mail van, which could easily have outpaced him. A bicycle, running so silently that every hoof fall sounded louder than gunfire, must have felt an inadequate means of escape.

I remembered my childhood gymnastics over the five-barred gate. If only the bureaucrat who organises mechanised postal services could be winkled out of his cushy office seat on to our mail bike saddle, we should get an earlier post. Even our quiet old Galloway bull would make the sparks shower off his pedals till he got back to his garage and issued himself a van!

# 27. Foiled

Miss Roedoe, our old tame deer, was so beautiful that she filled the most unimaginative eyes with her elegance and grace. She was as fond of the good things of life as the spoiled females of any other species, and came galloping out of the wood at the faintest rattle of a biscuit tin. She was a foundling that I had reared on the bottle and she was a great success. When she died, I decided to repeat the experiment by hand-rearing a kid bred by one of the other roe deer which shared her enclosure.

Such good resolutions are easier to make than to put into effect. Six acres of paddock and woodland and pool around our house are enclosed in a fox-proof fence and our roe deer have lived there for years. They are generally considered to be very difficult creatures to keep in enclosed places because they are delicate. I am particularly proud of ours because they have demonstrated their content by producing young five years out of the last six. Although they will come up to within a few yards of me for a bowl of flaked maize, they are still basically wild animals and Miss Roedoe was the only one which has ever let me touch her.

They normally drop their kids about the middle of May and it is always marvellous to me that they survive. The new-born kids are about as big as wild rabbits and their mothers leave them quite alone, lying in a 'form' or nest of grass or bracken, except when she visits to suckle them. This is because young kids are so fragile and tender that they stand a far better chance of survival lying hidden from their enemies than by trying to seek safety in flight.

By the time the bracken had recovered from frost and sprouted friendly fronds, the tussocky grass was lush enough to provide a comfortable couch of concealment. So a doe kidded on 1st June, about a fortnight after her expected time. I saw the kid before it was dry. Its mother was standing over it and licking its coat clean of the lubricant which had eased its birth. Then she gave it its first feed and left it alone, curled in the heart of a thick clump of grass.

Two days later, a television camera crew arrived to start work on a film about the wildlife here. They were delighted with the unexpected bonus of shots of a new-born roe kid, lying within a stone's throw of the study window.

I decided to leave it for about a week to gain strength and then to rear it by hand on the bottle as I had done with Miss Roedoe eleven years before. Such a task is a considerable tie. A bottle-reared kid simply has to be fed regularly. There is no question of holidays or days off or absence for any other reason until it is weaned in autumn. You have to be a glutton for punishment to embark on such a task. But nothing worthwhile is easy and my previous experience had taught me that the potential rewards far out-weighed the temporary inconvenience. It is possible to strike up a close friendship with deer that have been bottle-reared and lost their fear of man. In return, I could provide natural woodland for cover and food with the security of not being hounded by dogs, nor shot by men, which many wild deer must envy.

My eyes are as sharp as most and my experience as a practical naturalist has taught me how to use them. So you might think it would be easy for me to find something as big as a young deer in the restricted area around my house. I thought I knew exactly where the doe had left her kid – but a diligent search soon proved me wrong. So I set about quartering the area, yard by patient yard. I found two wild duck sitting on nests I hadn't even suspected, and several pheasants clapped so tight in tussocks that I nearly trod on them. The cocks were the shade of russet I was looking for in the kid and I could have spat at them in disappointment every time they proved me wrong. I found birds' nests and owl pellets and a colony of bank voles living in a pile of logs we'd cut and stored for winter. I found several depressions in the grass where the kid had recently been lying-up. But I didn't find the kid.

I repeated the search each day until I'd convinced myself that she must have died from cold and wet – but I didn't find the corpse either. I would hate to admit how many hours I wasted in this fruitless quest before I eventually stumbled on her by accident rather than by skill. I was overjoyed and stopped to pick her up and feast my eyes on her beauty. I had never thought of the kid as anything but 'her' because I'd never really contemplated failure. But when I held her in my arms I realised she was not 'her' but 'him'. The kid I had searched for so patiently was a little buck and utterly useless for rearing by hand.

This is because male deer, all male deer when they become adult, are very dangerous if they lose their fear and respect for man. They are as aggressive as other entire males and quite as savage and treacherous as the worst bull or stallion. They attack not only with their antlers, but with sharp hooves as well. And once started, they go on attacking in spite of the fact that their does are the most affectionate and delightful creatures when tame and confident.

So I knew it was no good taking my little roe buck. Although he would never be bigger than a fair-sized dog, he could easily castrate a man. I admired his youthful innocence for a few seconds and put him gently back in the form where he had successfully hidden so long. He would never lose his natural wildness and become bold enough to attack if I left him to be reared by his mother, but he would still provide colour and movement and endless interest for years to come.

So I added him to the long list of my good resolutions which never quite came off.

# 28. Getting a wife on a bit of string

The cattle byre at the far end of our wood is a hive of activity all winter. Its centres of attraction are the bin of cattle nuts in one corner and the hay racks which line the walls. However unpalatable these nuts might seem to human palates, cattle and sheep jostle for them with the ill-mannered ardour of ravenous schoolboys. So do the Bagot goats.

When the stately home season is over and Blithfield Hall is closed to the public, the Bagot goats return here to the woods where their ancestors roamed wild for more than six centuries. They spend their days grazing in peace on Daffodil Lawn, but they always keep a watchful eye open for the dogs and me coming through the wood. The first to spot us dashes to get head of the queue for the hay and nuts that I dole out.

Goats are greedy creatures with appetites as omnivorous as ostriches, so that it is vital to take the utmost care to strip off every strand of string which binds the hay into compressed rectangles. It might choke them if they swallowed it. To avoid the chance of such a catastrophe through any fault of mine, I loop each strand of twine well out of harm's way over the beams in the roof. The byre is cool and deserted in summer, so shady it provides a perfect sanctuary from intrusion.

Two years ago I was delighted to find a bird's nest woven into the hanks of twine I had left hanging there some months ago. It was a spherical nest, about the size of a croquet ball, with an entrance hole at the side as big as a two penny bit. The nest itself was woven from carefully matched fibres and leaves and mosses. It had also been cunningly incorporated into the hanging strings so that it was suspended with deceptive strength. Many people part with hard-earned cash to go on conducted safaris to foreign lands without seeing anything half as beautifully fashioned.

I tapped the beam gently with my forefinger in the hope that I should get a glimpse of the tenant as she left the nest. Nothing happened so I gingerly touched the supporting strings. Still nothing came out, so I poked a questing forefinger through the entrance hole. The nest had been finished with superb craftsmanship and softly lined but the hen

The wren's nest in the binder twine

bird had not yet laid her clutch of eggs, so I returned a week later with no better luck.

From the shape and size of the nest I knew that a wren had built it and that it was quite possible that no eggs would ever be laid there, nor fledglings hatched. When this happens, country folk say that it is a cock nest and this is literally true. It is the cock wren who decides which building site will be the most perfect for a nest. When he has chosen the spot, he builds a residence which he hopes will steal the heart of some attractive hen, and if he is not successful he builds yet another nest and tries again.

Apart from the goldcrest, he is the tiniest English bird and his colour is not in the least flamboyant but sober brown. But, in common with most small people, he has a voice out of all proportion to his size. He sings a very loud song indeed and he repeats it, not so much as a token of a joyous heart as a warning to other cock wrens that this is his territory and that they trespass at their peril. A fringe benefit of such melody is that hen wrens in search of love know where to look for a mate with the self-confidence to believe that he really has something to shout about. Any hen who comes within his territory is given a conducted tour of nests he has built in the hopes that she will consent to settle down and raise a brood in one of them.

For reasons best known to themselves, no prospective mate was bowled over by the quality of the nest woven into the string hanging in our byre two years ago. Perhaps the situation was too dark or there was some flaw in construction not obvious to me. Maybe a butt of grass stuck out uncomfortably where it should have been tucked in. Or the minor movements of the hanging string might have imparted a sense of insecurity to birds more used to nests packed into the crevices of walls, or between the solid branches of a tree. Whatever the fault, the nest was still hanging there unoccupied when the goats returned in autumn.

I was naturally disappointed so I deliberately draped another bunch of binder twine over the same beam last year. I do not know if the old cock wren risked failure twice or if another bird was attracted by the same location. Whatever the case, another beautiful nest was built, but no hen came to lay there.

The third time was lucky. This year a nest appeared as usual, though

I had no great hopes that it would be occupied. I am glad that I was wrong. Perhaps persistence won in the end and a reluctant hen could not for shame refuse such dogged determination. Or perhaps nesting fashions changed and secret nests in shady spots have become the in-thing with with-it wrens.

At last the nest in the byre has a family of healthy chicks but I am wondering if success has also bred success. Cock wrens do not build several nests in their territory only out of a chivalrous motive of giving their wives a choice of residence. Given the chance, cock wrens might be polygamous and like nothing better than a seductive hen in every nest. I have a sneaking suspicion that his accomplishments may have gone to our old bird's head and that the little hen in our byre may be only one of his harem.

# 29. Holidays at home

The bats in my belfry occasionally break loose. Just once in a while, a subconscious spendthrift urge explodes in the back of my mind and propels me on a wild shopping spree. The complaint is commoner with women than men, as anyone would agree who has been an involuntary fleck of flotsam buffeted through a city store at Christmas time. I limit such urban expeditions to the bi-monthly visits when I am forced to get my hair cut but, alas, it is not necessary to go to be skint of hard-earned brass.

I never go on holidays abroad because steamships make me sick and aeroplanes frighten me. The idea of being cooped up on a humid summer night in a sweaty caravan fills me with nausea and coach tours would bore me stiff. My tastes are so simple that it is dangerously easy to be filled with smug self-satisfaction at the extravagance of others. But I am not the paragon that such sentiments imply; my vices simply take a different course. I manage to kid myself that I get better value for my money. Whatever your views are on such opinions, there is no doubt about the arithmetic. One year we persuaded ourselves that we could get immense creative satisfaction by bulldozing an island in our pool. We got the island for less than our passage in a boat to Majorca and we enjoy it every day instead of trying to recapture memories while we bore our friends with holiday snaps.

My extravagance this year is of less certain value. Our bird table is made from an old grindstone from a corn mill, mounted on three rick staddles. It is four feet across and attracts a constant stream of visitors right up to the sitting-room window. I have long coveted a bird bath of similar generous proportions. At first it was a vague subconscious craving, and I convinced myself that a bird bath outside my study window would match the bird table and add an air of symmetry.

If you have never tried to buy a bird bath four feet wide, I must warn you that everyone you ask will glance furtively over his shoulder to make sure of his way of escape. Just in case you really are a nutter. I tried to get another millstone which could be hollowed out to hold the water, but millstones are as scarce as diamonds – and about as expensive. So I asked all my friends to look out for one for me, and someone in Herefordshire offered me a complete cider mill about ten feet across which would have needed a low loader to transport and would have dwarfed the cottage when it arrived.

I importuned unsuspecting farmers with the effrontery of a knocker in the antique trade and every miller for miles around must have been sick at the sight of me. So far I had searched only for a stone which had served its original purpose; something that had become a white elephant which the owner might be relieved to turn into cash.

As the quest grew demonstrably more futile, it dawned on me that the only hope was to open my purse, shake out the moths and lash out regardless. I still tried to kid myself that this would be no more expensive than other people's holidays, but the guff about enjoying watching a bird bath long after the memory of beach bathing beauties lost their charms was not convincing.

Then I remembered that the cover of one book I wrote had a badger at my window and the cover of the next book showed Miss Roedoe, my tame roe deer, calling at the same window for elevenses. A colour picture of a bird bath to end all bird baths, full of splashing rarities in front of this window, would make the perfect trilogy. That my next book would be a non-starter without such a monument on its cover seemed a logical conclusion.

I eventually discovered a quarry at Hollington where the stone to build our house came from a century and a half ago. When I arrived, the masons were carving superb pinnacles for St Peter's, Wolverhampton. Colin Shaw, the boss, was not only a master mason, he was the calibre of sales psychologist who has no difficulty in persuading customers who call for four-foot bird baths that they are normal and the rest of the world is odd. Before I knew what had hit me, my spending spree was over – and I had bought myself a Christmas box which turned out far cheaper than I had any right to expect.

It weighs nearly two tons so Colin didn't exaggerate when he remarked that it would take a fairly big bird to tip it over. Domestic pigeons and shy wild birds are equally addicted to its comforts. They fill the air outside my study with droplets which shimmer into rainbows in the sunlight, as brilliant as on the most romantic tropical island.

# 30. Delightful Sprite

Our young fallow deer arrived with us five weeks ago today – and I am only just beginning to win the battle for her affections. She came as a fawn which had been picked up in a deer park where her ancestors had spent generations in semi-captivity confined by a deer fence. They had never been hunted nor harried by poachers, and in times of exceptionally hard weather, there had always been a keeper to eke out their rations with sweet hay or potatoes. Domestic cattle and sheep had shared the 200 or 300 acres where they had been free to roam. Their placid presence could have been expected to calm irrational fears to which truly wild animals are so often subject.

Honey, having overcome her initial fear, is quite at home at Goat Lodge

In theory, therefore, my young deer should have been simple enough to rear and she ought to have grown up as tame and stolid as a milk cow. Such theories rarely work out in practice. This young creature had been picked up at about ten or fourteen days old and brought to me. She was no ordinary fawn. Her mother was white and it is already obvious from the way her baby coat is fading that she too will moult out white when she grows up. Instead of being brown or dun, with dappled spots, she is a uniform ginger with the faintest hint of white undercoat.

The reason that she came to me was that the owner of the herd does not like abnormal colouration so that she might have been culled for venison if I hadn't rescued her. I was delighted to welcome her. My old tame roe deer which recently died aged ten was the most attractive and beautiful wild creature I ever tamed. I was happy to replace her by another deer, but this time I thought I'd rear a fallow fawn when the only roe kid available turned out to be a buck.

Although there are lots of wild fallow deer in our wood, I still know less about their private lives than I do about the roe deer which I have kept for more than a decade. It wasn't until this latest fawn arrived though, that I realised the depth of my ignorance.

Instead of being as simple as a lamb to rear, this prima donna proved as difficult as any foundling which ever landed on our doorstep. She flew into blind panic if I flicked so much as an eyelid and bucketted round, banging into whatever barred her path. So my first chore was to line a small outbuilding with smooth wall board which would cushion any self-inflicted knocks without being rough enough to graze her tender flesh.

The moment my shadow darkened her door she stiffened with apprehension and both of us benefitted from my years of experience in handling wild animals. I always managed to intercept her dive for freedom by catching her as a wicket keeper fields a ball, before she could do herself injury. She screamed as piteously as a wounded hare and then subsided limp in my arms as she tasted the sweet warm milk in her bottle.

If you cannot conquer a wild creature without breaking its spirit it would be wicked to try. I suppose she could have been starved into submission, but such victory would taste no better than sawdust. My experience is that the only satisfactory way to produce a deep and lasting bond of affection which is mutual is by kindness. It has taken almost infinite patience but I have at last managed to win her heart by gentling her.

There are tricks, of course, in every trade and I had to convince her first that I am harmless by iron self-discipline in never making any sudden movement. When she trusted the fact that I was not stalking her, nor in any other way plotting her harm, I had broken the ice. The next step after conquering her mental foreboding was more positive. It was vital that she should associate my approach with physical pleasure. I did this in two ways. One was the bottle with its taste and smell of her precious milk, and the other was careful grooming.

Young fawns get obvious delight from feeding but they seem to get an even more intense ecstasy from their mother's gentle grooming which produces a reflex action that prompts them to empty themselves while they are actually feeding. In the wild, this is vital for survival. If they left their droppings around them where they slept, foxes or other predators would hunt them by scent. So her instinct makes the doe stimulate them to leave their telltale taint away from the spot where they will lie hidden when she leaves them.

The fact that I knew her intimate secrets helped me to break down her suspicion so that the fawn now trusts me and is no longer frightened. Instead of cowering when I come, she gets up when she hears my voice and trots to meet me. With at least half-an-hour in her company four times a day for a month, it is not surprising that we now know each other pretty well.

The next stage was to accustom her to strangers and Anne Moonie helped me here. She was at our local girls' boarding school and spent as much of her spare time with us as she could, as her sister Liz did until she left. Anne liked to join me when I fed the fawn and she managed to convince it that other human beings can be kind and friendly too. With luck and management, it will grow up into the most beautiful white doe and I hope to give her her freedom in the wood. I hope that, because of her outstanding colour, everyone around will know her and refrain from harming her.

The one snag we cannot agree about is a suitable name for her. When

I was a boy, I used to stay on an estate which had rather a gruesome ghost story. The squire had for years been trying fruitlessly to produce an heir but, just when his wife was obviously that way inclined, she contracted smallpox. When the squire asked his doctor if the coveted child would catch the disease, he was told it could only be avoided by a very dangerous operation. The decision was his. "Cut down the tree to spare the branch," the father said. And the child lived at the expense of his mother's life. The murdered wife has haunted the park ever since, wandering around in the form of a white fallow deer.

The story etched itself into my mind so that I wanted to call my white fawn Spook, because I hope to see her white shape drifting through our wood in the moonlight. Our friends were horrified at the idea of calling such a dainty sprite an eerie name, so we compromised with Honey. Her coat isn't *quite* white, so honey describes her accurately by day. But by silver moonlight a ghost by any other name is still a spook to me!

# 31. Making pigs of themselves

Among a magnum of memories of a misspent youth are idle days on the river at Oxford. A pleasant stretch of water and its grassy banks had been enclosed by an elaborate fence. This was set aside for bathing and strictly reserved for men only, who were not required to wear costumes of any sort. It was known as Parson's Pleasure!

Females in boats passing up and down the river had to get out when they reached the spot and footslog round the peep-proof fence to wait for their boats to emerge on the other side. Spirited wenches resented this and there was great competition to be the first girl to sail through undetected. Punts were piled high with cushions of concealment and slim maidens donned beards and false moustaches to impersonate their betters.

But the attendants were so skilled at detecting such deceptions that most invaders were unceremoniously decanted. When the occasional one did breach the defences, she was soon spotted and the banks heaved with manly bodies stampeding for the water faster than panicking seals. The affronted sunbathers swam straight for the intruders, capsized their boat and tipped them into the water – cushions, clothes, disguise and all. Few returned to take another peep.

The day that sticks out most in my memory was untrammelled by such incidents. The sky was blue, the summer air was filled with birdsong – and the scorching sun was pitiless. I basked as indolent as a lizard until my tummy tingled, and then rolled over to tan my back. When that tingled too, I plunged into the crystal water to cool off, and then repeated the process in the belief that I should be transformed into a sunbronzed Adonis.

The mountains of masculinity sprawled on the grass around should have dispelled such illusions. Their uncouth figures were as raw and red as beefsteak on a butcher's slab and, when I returned to my lodgings, I realised just how sore I was. It was agony to lie on my back and worse to lie on my front so that I did not get a wink of sleep for nights.

Time is a wonderful healer and I never gave it another thought until a couple of weeks ago when this year's bunch of pigs arrived. I keep pigs during the summer and autumn to make clearings in the wood where I can grow buckwheat and rape and turnips to attract the deer and birds to feed.

When I went to buy this year's pigs, I got deep satisfaction by giving them their freedom in my large enclosure of natural woodland where they could wander freely as their ancestors used to do. They cavorted round and grunted with pleasure. They ploughed deep furrows with their powerful leathery snouts. They rooted by instinct for titbits undreamed of in the fetid sweat box where they might otherwise have been imprisoned.

Quite soon they slowed and tired because they were unaccustomed to such exercise. I had made them a water-proof shelter and stuffed it with soft straw, but they stretched out instead and basked in the scorching sunlight, reminding me of the prostrate bodies on the banks of the river at Oxford. All animals love comfort and these pigs found the same delight in lying at ease in the warmth as we had in my youth. The sight of them should have jogged my memory of what happens to 'mad dogs and Englishmen who go out in the midday sun'.

Next day they were stretched out asleep in the sun, but when they heard the rattle of my bucket they came towards me. I noticed that one only walked a few steps before hollowing his back until his belly almost touched the ground. It was as if he was stooping to creep beneath an invisible bramble or strand of barbed wire which he was excessively careful to negotiate without touching.

Then I noticed others cutting the same caper, apparently avoiding obstacles which weren't there. Their white skins had turned as red as lobsters and even their ears were skinning. The poor creatures were suffering from sunburn and I was filled with fellow feeling.

Pigs are exceptionally susceptible to sunburn, especially predominantly white pigs, but they have a natural defence against it. Mud! In hot weather, they love to wallow in a mudbath, and countryfolk who know about such things say that they are 'happy as pigs in muck'. Those who disparage them as 'dirty pigs' simply display their ignorance. Pigs love mud which is not dirty but is simply clean water mixed with honest earth.

So I flooded a hollow of heavy clay in the wood and enjoyed the pleasure they derived from it as much as they did. They lay in the shallow water first, to ease their sunburn, as we had cooled off in the river at Parson's Pleasure. Then they rooted below the surface, blowing bubbles from their snouts which clouded the water with silt. Their little cloven hooves cut into the bottom of the puddle, creaming the water with mud and, as they continued to loosen more soil, the liquid thickened into black custard. When they had achieved the precise consistency they like, they lay down gingerly with grunts and sighs of satisfaction.

No ageing beauty beneath the mudpack in her exclusive salon got more effective therapy. The mud eased their sunburn and dried into a film which filtered out a second dose. Thus coated, they can now lie out in rows to cook like ladies in a lido. The difference is that they know how to take their pleasures harmlessly instead of getting as sunburned as a pig's ear!

# 32. The goose that played gooseberry

My desk has recently been the centre of an eternal feathered triangle. In theory, I spend several hours a day scratching a living with my pen. But for the last week, or so, my thoughts have been distracted by a plot which has unfolded that owes nothing to my inspiration.

An earlier episode of the drama of our Canada geese can be read in **Island of Enchantment**. All went well till we felled a tree by the pool at the end of January. It was a large oak and the chain saw's yowl was disturbing enough. The hubbub when the tree cracked was the last straw. The geese flew away very low down the valley out of view. They flew so low they couldn't get proper bearings. So I was not surprised

The successful Canada Goose on her nest

when they failed to return. I thought they were lost. Disappointing, but not unexpected. It is easy to frighten wild creatures away, but difficult to persuade them to settle where you want.

The pool remained quiet until February when a pair of wild geese arrived and took possession. I didn't pay much attention because I thought they were the usual pair which would hang around for a few weeks, be thoroughly objectionable to later arrivals, and then spurn my hospitality by clearing off to nest elsewhere. Not a bit of it. They have scarcely left the place since they arrived and the goose has laid a clutch of eggs at the far end of the pool which she is now incubating.

I am not too optimistic about her prospects because we had two very hard frosts after she laid but before she started to sit. So the eggs may have been frosted before she was sitting on them to protect them. Anyhow, the gander dreams his days away on the pool and is only galvanised into action if he hears the voice of other geese. They are not 'our' pair of geese, but it was very nice to have them all the same.

I say was because this is where the plot has thickened. Soon after the resident goose had gone broody and settled on her eggs, we were awakened at dawn by a trumpeting which would surely have toppled the walls of Jericho. I leaped out of bed and could see, in the gathering light, a number of geese engaged in what was obviously the father-and-mother of all domestic brawls. When it grew lighter, I distinguished two pairs of geese disputing possession of our pool and paddock. I was surprised to see an odd man out as well. Odd girl out, to be more accurate, as I later discovered.

I examined the interlopers through my field glasses and saw that two were the ones which had been reared here and the third was a stranger. I knew that two were 'ours' because, although I normally disapprove of ringing wild birds because of risks involved, I had made an exception with them. I had fitted a light plastic ring to the right leg of each gosling so that if they did fly away I might get news of them if they were recaptured or shot. Two of the birds which had trumpeted us out of our sleep were wearing my white rings, so I knew they were our last year's goslings.

I now found the strangers who were incubating eggs less welcome. I wished they hadn't come so 'ours' would have been free to nest. There was nothing I could do about it. So I settled down to watch the plot develop.

In the first scene the residents drove 'our' pair and their new companion away. But they seemed so glad to have found 'home' again that they were immensely persistent and returned time after time – always sparking off another noisy quarrel. Then I noticed a refinement in the plot.

I had assumed 'our' goslings were a pair because one was slightly larger than the other. Sex differences may be obvious enough to other geese, but they were not to me. I now saw that the newcomer without a plastic ring was definitely larger than our ringed birds and it was obvious he was the gander.

The behaviour of the odd-girl-out was interesting too. At first, when the resident gander drove off the interlopers, she went too, a pathetic unwanted gooseberry, always squeezed out of their circle. But they were so objectionable to her that she eventually slunk back to our paddock, a spinster driven home when her sister takes up with a boy friend. Not unnaturally, the resident gander saw in her less of a threat than from another mated pair so he was less aggressive.

If he does harass her now she simply retreats to my study window sill where no wild goose dare approach because of his natural fear of man. She has spent so much time there this week she seems to have forgotten she ever flew away to the wild. She was very fond of us and the dogs as a gosling and now she seems to have developed a crush on the dogs. When she is not actively grazing, she is separated from them only by the thickness of the glass. When the dogs go into the paddock she follows like a shadow.

But I do not think that will be the end of the story. The gander on the pool is going to be forced to live a bachelor life for a month while his goose is incubating her eggs. I notice that already he is not as assiduous in harassing the spinster goose as he quite naturally is with a strange gander. He is already beginning to allow her to go down to drink and bathe. She may not remain forever uncomely in his eyes!

Watching this drama at close range makes me feel like an avian agony columnist. I feel already qualified to write a column specialising in feathered matrimonial problems. And if I had to earn a living by uncoupling triangles I should try to convince the goose that there are as many good birds in the sky as were ever shot out of it. I should warn her that getting ideas about dogs will be rated 'queer' by all rightminded geese!

# Autumn

# 33. A magic day in autumn

I can lie in bed and look up the woodland ride across the paddock at the first glint of dawn. It is a lovely view in any season, but at the tag-end of October and the first week of November it is superb. There is often just enough swirling white mist to soften the outline of the trees, giving the illusion that they are part of a cathedral nave. The ground slopes up into the distance. The red ball of the rising sun is as brilliant as a stained glass window.

As I looked out the other morning, a fallow deer, jet black in silhouette against the sun, moved towards me with all the dignity of an ancient monk. The temptation to lie snug and warm, savouring the best of both worlds by watching the cold dawn from my warm blankets, was easy to resist. So I tumbled out of bed to go for a walk with Tick, my German pointer.

I would rather tramp the countryside with her than almost any human being. She knows every inch of our ground as intimately as I do;

**Fallow deer in a beautiful autumnal setting**

she knows where the moles tunnel close beneath the surface of the woodland rides, which trees the squirrels climb most frequently and where the pheasants feed. She always returns hopefully to those spots, and she 'points' her latest discovery out to me. She is the perfect companion for a country walk. What my dull senses would never discover are an open book to her acute eyes and ears and nose.

Dogs are so intelligent that they remember for months, and sometimes years, the precise spot where they found a rabbit or pheasant. They never pass the place again without making certain that they are missing nothing. This can develop into a very bad fault. While they are concentrating on an obsolete hiding place, they may fail to discover something new.

So I like to take Tick as often as possible to strange country, uncluttered by pre-conceived hopes, where she must use her initiative to unravel each strange scent. The air was so crisp and the autumn colours so beautiful the other morning that I telephoned a friend who is head keeper on a great estate. I asked if I could come over with my bitch for a walk in his domain. He welcomed me with open arms.

The parkland rolled gently as an ocean swell away from the Big House. A horseshoe lake, at precisely the right spot to give deep perspective, curved out of sight into an oak wood. A herd of deer were guzzling sweet chestnuts almost before they spilled from the tree. The open parkland was dotted with little spinneys of larch and spruce, carefully sited on the sides of the hills. Pheasants could be concentrated here by regular feeding and driven over guns placed deep in the valleys below. They would provide most difficult targets and give the birds a sporting chance.

But such little coverts were not laid out only for pheasant shooting or foxhunting. They were accurately sited to provide aesthetically satisfying views, and their carefully chosen trees can never be seen to greater advantage than in autumn time. No artist could commit such beauty to canvas for the simple reason that it is never static. The subtle shades of yellow, amber, ochre, red, russet and green could never blend so wonderfully without their gentle movement in the breeze.

Movement, I think, was the key to the whole of that magic day. Trees, reflected in the lake, were never still. The wind constantly shifted the water surface, and a flock of wild mallard, flighting and playing in the sunlight, let loose an infinity of ripples. The birds themselves were not specially exciting in the distance, but I was able to creep close up to them under cover of a reed bed. Then I could see the irridescent greens of their heads, and necks almost as brilliant as a kingfisher's. It contrasted with the subdued greys and browns and the blue on their wings. I couldn't help thinking that folk who travel in discomfort to foreign lands to see exotic birds are chucking away their money.

A man was ploughing on the edge of the park and the wizened straw stubble writhed behind him to leave furrows of rich brown soil. I stopped to pick up a handful for the sensual pleasure of feeling next season's fertility crumble through my fingers. I can never appreciate beauty to the full with one sense on its own. The sight of autumn woods is always sharpened by the smell of fallen leaves. And the song of a blackbird is never so mellow if I can't see the sheen on his feathers or the praise pouring from his yellow bill.

Such splendour bears no relationship to rarity. My friend is an artist at persuading game to flourish, and his brilliant cock pheasants swaggered arrogant in every ride. They gleaned the remaining grain and strutted over new-turned soil in search of worms and insects the plough had dispossessed. The brilliance of their colours delighted my eyes and their scent intoxicated Tick. But she didn't disgrace me. She was equally restrained at the sight of fallow deer in the park, and hares on the open plough. She made me swell with pride at her good manners, and I couldn't resist the temptation to ask my friend for his opinion.

He is a kind fellow, full of enthusiasm and generous with his compliments. He said that he saw plenty of keeper-worked dogs who couldn't hold a candle to her. He made the autumn colours twice as bright in my eyes. The pheasants never looked so fat, nor sky so blue. I don't know when I enjoyed a walk so much.

# 34. A game register of rarities

Keen shooting men have always kept a record of their bags so that the game books of old estates are often of great value to modern naturalists. I have listened to papers read by learned scientists who had relied for their information almost exclusively on such records. They can be an accurate yardstick, for example, to the fluctuations in numbers of the creatures whose sudden death they record. The number of pheasants or partridges shot in a season is likely to bear some relation to the stock of game that year.

So, if the game book shows a 'bad' season, when few partridges were shot, a study of the weather charts for the same year may well disclose that mid-June was wet. This is the period when partridge chicks are most vulnerable to cold and damp, so they probably died of natural causes long before they were old enough to be shot in flight.

If there was no obvious reason, the detective work involved in deducing the real cause of the decline is a mental exercise that naturalists find more stimulating than any game of chess.

Game books usually had columns for pheasant and partridge, grouse, blackgame, deer, rabbits, hares and duck. The right-hand column bore the title 'various'. This covered a multitude of sins as well as a rag-bag of oddities. Cats and foxes were left undefined except as 'various' for obvious reasons. But our forefathers had no such scruples about admitting to the execution of a whole range of hawks and owls and badgers, and other creatures they counted as vermin.

The heyday of such records coincided with the Victorian era of collecting bric-a-brac. Ladies filled prissy cabinets with polished shells and curios and ornamental china. Men lined their billiard room walls with glass cases of stuffed rarities. Albino crows and stoats rubbed shoulders with beautiful barn owls and kingfishers. Pine martens and sandy-coloured badgers played on banks of artificial grass. Some of these creatures were trapped by gamekeepers or shot by collectors. A great many breathed their last fresh air the day before their names appeared in the 'various' column of a game book.

So game books are not only useful to follow the fluctuating fortunes of common creatures; they are often as important as transactions of the local field club or natural history society for a census of visitors rarely seen.

Last week a shooting party saw a bird swimming on the pool near Abbots Bromley which they 'thought was a snipe or teal'. When it rose to fly away, the nearest sportsman made it pay the penalty of getting airborne. I imagine it was brought to me so that I could tell them under what title they should enter it in the 'various' column of their game book. It was a bird I had never seen before, looking a bit like a puffin but with white wing bars on its dark plumage and white cheeks. So it obviously wasn't a puffin. Its webbed feet were set far back, as in most birds created to dive and swim under water more than walk on land, and it was small enough almost to lie in the palm of my hand.

I was ignorant of what it was so I looked it up, to find that it was a Little Auk, or sea-dove, an oceanic bird which breeds on sheltered rocks in the Arctic. It is the smallest of the sea-diving birds and when it leaves its Arctic breeding grounds, it still hangs around the pack ice, feeding on plankton and crustaceans and small fish. Occasionally these lovely little birds are caught up in a gale and blown miles off course. Some years they arrive in such battered parties that they are called 'wrecks' of Auks. Wreck is an unfortunately apt description because they have little chance of surviving to reach the open Arctic seas again. Yet the bird that was brought to me had not been in bad condition. Its plummage was glossy, and it was fat. I gathered that, when first seen, it was swimming strongly on the pool. I have no means of knowing how long it had been fending for itself so far inland, but there hadn't been a wind strong enough to earn the title gale for some time. Perhaps, if it had had the luck to choose some unshot pool like mine, it might still be going strong. It is a pity it had to end its days as an entry in a game book, with its obituary on this page.

It does raise the question of how rare is a rarity. So far as birds are concerned, especially birds that frequent large sheets of water, there is practically no chance at all of a rarity escaping notice. Certainly, if it is bold enough to show its beak at the weekend. The population of bird-watchers is denser round reservoirs than almost anywhere else. This is partly a matter of access. All you need is a pair of powerful field glasses and one spot where you can legally approach the water's edge, and every species there can be ticked off on your checklist.

On land there is more cover so that it is only possible to see one small area at a time, and the owner may well object to your wandering there anyway. Scores of fascinating birds probably go unsung in such places for the simple reason that nobody sees them who is equipped to recognise them. The lovely waterside birds like ruffs and reeves and osprey and rare waders are lucky. They get their names in the bird notes of their local bird clubs or natural history societies.

It is a far pleasanter place to be written-up than in the 'various' column of a game book, because they live to fly another day and to delight more than the original chap who spotted them.

# 35. Toads by the thousand

My annual letter from the man from Crabbery Street puts me in mind
of Moses. Improbable as it may sound, Crabbery Street really was the
address of my local Inspector of Taxes. When he sent his demand for
his cut of what meagre profit I make as a naturalist, I wondered how he
would have got on with Moses and his brother.

It is quite plain from the Book of Exodus, that Moses was a much
better naturalist than I am. He turned Aaron's rod into a serpent, and
produced swarms of flies at his command; he made the river run with
blood and the earth crawl with lice and afflicted the Egyptian cattle
with a sort of foot-and-mouth disease called murrain.

I covet most his power of producing swarms of frogs. He conjured
them up in such abundance that they came into the houses and
bedchambers and upon the beds. Imagine the glorious havoc they
would wreak among the computers of Crabbery Street! The odd thing
is that the tale is not as far fetched as it seems.

Dr Robert Plot, who wrote the *Natural History of Staffordshire* in 1686,
believed that frogs sometimes descended in showers of rain and he
describes them falling so thick on a bowling green at Tixall, near Stafford, that it was impossible to walk without treading on them.

One ancient theory was that 'the spawn or seed' of frogs was blown
from the tops of mountains or sucked up from the earth with water
vapour, brought to perfection in the clouds and discharged thence in
showers. Plot himself thought that they were produced on the surface of
the earth or on the tops of houses 'by fermentation excited by dust'. If
he had been with me the other night, he might have thought the good
old days were back.

The concrete farm track that goes past our wood was literally
crawling not with frogs but toads. Unfortunately, both are getting
scarcer because the little pools they love to breed in are being filled-in
by farmers who find corn more profitable than duckweed. So toads by
the thousand as I saw them the other night are a welcome sight indeed.

My toads did not rain down from heaven like the biblical frogs or
those on Tixall bowling green. They crawled up from our pool. It

covers an acre and a half and used to be a famous place for pike. There must have been plenty of fish in those days to feed the pike, and the fish would eat the tadpoles. Now it has silted up with oak leaves, it is too acid for fish to thrive. But there are yellow flags round the edge and reeds and bog bean, so that there is plenty of cover and minute food. In spring, the air groans with the croaking of coupled toads so that the water wriggles later with tadpoles.

At this time of year, they leave the water to hibernate, but are uncomfortable if their skins get too dry. They love the moisture of dewy nights to move so that the real time to see them is during the first shower after a dry spell. They then yield to the compulsive urge to swarm to places where they will be cool enough for their animation to be suspended, but not cold enough to freeze.

The other night, they were crossing our drive as thick as a cup-tie football crowd, oblivious alike of traffic or predators. It isn't easy to discover where so many quite large creatures find to skulk away the winter in safety. I have turned them up under tree roots half a mile from the pool and deep in the mud under reeds at the water's edge. I have found them in cellars and drains, and under stones on the rockery. Some of the places they squeeze into are so incredibly small that the ancients believed they could penetrate solid rock.

According to Dr Plot, when the steeple of Stafford church was taken down to prevent it falling, the top stone of the spire split as it hit the ground and – you've guessed it – a live toad came out. He said that another as big as a man's fist was found twelve feet up in a oak tree at Lapley, and there was one in the centre of a tree at Walsall which died when exposed to air.

Sceptics may think that splitting the steeple stone or felling trees disturbed toads nearby and that it was just faulty deduction to assume they had been there all the time. Dr Plot said that, being cold-blooded, toads did not perspire, so losing no heat, they needed no energy to replace it.

Fire and water have an irresistible attraction for boys of all ages. So I mooned away much of my youth on the banks of pools and canals, catching tadpoles and frogs, and toads and newts. They are such mysterious creatures that superstitions about them come as natural as the boyish urge to capture them. We called newts 'wet efts' or 'askers' and we didn't just believe they spat fire. We were as certain of it as the smoke that belched out of the nostrils of St George's dragon.

So why should we now doubt that a toad can live a century in a block of solid stone? After seeing my swarm of toads the other night, I no longer snigger at the stories of the plague of frogs which Moses and Aaron called down on Pharaoh's head. With luck, they may rain down on Crabbery Street before April 5 next year!

# 36. Fun with pheromones

I have never managed to test the theory that women with red hair smell like foxes. I did not have the luck to have a redhead on my list of dancing partners when I was young. Now, alas, I am too old for such frolics. In any case, it was among the fantasies that I wrote off as old wives' tales, designed to deter old men from straying.

Recent research has thrown new light on the whole subject of the effect that scent has upon behaviour. An International Congress of Pure and Applied Chemistry held in Boston examined the question of pheromones. That is the scientific jargon for chemicals secreted to induce a physiological response of other individuals of the same species, and the scientists have at last tumbled to their real significance.

If you have a bitch in season, you don't need a scientist to tell you that the scent she leaves behind induces powerful physiological responses in

A female emperor moth

the dogs in the neighbourhood. They will move mountains to be near her. And the old tom, caterwauling on your tiles, did not receive a formal invitation.

The Pure Chemists have been back-slapping each other in mutual congratulation about a pheromone moth trap they have dreamed-up that also relies on scent. Gipsy moths were foolishly introduced from Europe about a century ago and their caterpillars recently killed a million American trees. 'Safe' poisons' proved ineffective against them and even the scientists were getting worried about the cumulative effects of their persistent pesticides. They calculate present risks to crops a lesser evil.

Dr Morris Beroza, whose job is agricultural research, told the conference about an alternative. It is a pheromone designed to prevent the moths from breeding without polluting the environment. This is not a method of chemical sterilisation but rather the reverse. It is the moth's own sex attractant and the scientists have discovered a formula for making the substance synthetically.

When they put a few grammes of this concoction on a wick inside a cylinder, the male gypsy moths flock in compulsively to their last blind date. The wily scientists paint the cylinder with the sticky stuff they put on old-fashioned fly papers so the moths cannot fly out when they discover they have been duped. This compels the virgin females to stay that way because of their prospective partners' fatal attraction to a pheromone fly trap. So the next generation must fail for lack of fathers.

An alternative method of using such scents is to scatter them widely over the whole area instead of concentrating them in traps. The poor male moths no longer fly into their sticky doom, but die of frustrated confusion instead. The whole air reeks of seduction and they exhaust themselves in a fruitless search for a diamond amongst the deceptive dross.

Although the discovery of pheromones – and especially how to make them synthetically – is new, ordinary amateur naturalists have been aware for years that moths attract their mates by scent. When I was at school, we used to put a female emperor moth in a jar with a perforated lid. The heady scent she exuded so filled the air that the eager male emperors congregated from great distances in the vain hope of the chance of making love. We had no idea that our moth's attractant scent would one day be called a pheromone, but we were well aware that her odour was sexually irresistible to her amorous suitors.

A month from now, our wood will reverberate to the courtship serenade of fallow deer. Each master buck will take his stand, and mark out his territory by fraying, or thrashing, the trees with his antlers. He will groan a challenge to his rivals and tell all the does, by the same song, that he awaits their pleasure. It is a language that we can understand because it comes natural to us to plead our love by word of mouth, but female deer have other ways of getting the message.

Ducts below the buck's eyes exude a scent – a pheromone, I suppose it is – that taints the trees he frays on. He underlines his exhortations by digging shallow scrapes around the edge of his territory and leaving in them the scent of his urine and semen. The combined effect of the whole ritual is to make the other bucks feel unwanted and to provide a powerful aphrodisiac for the does.

Buck stoats, at cliquetting time, travel miles for their mates, and keepers know that they leave clues of their prescence on stakes in hedgerows in the same way that town dogs record their token on every lamp post they pass. The old keepers have trapped such spots for years and could have taught the Pure Chemists of Boston most things about pheromones except the name.

Dog foxes blaze their trail in the same way and their scent is obviously attractive to other species too. The other night, my lurcher Spider rolled with delight on the spot in a woodland ride where I had seen a fox stop a few hours before. A pupil of Dr Freud said our powers of smell would be potentially as sensitive as a dog's but that we have subconsciously repressed them because smells are not considered aesthetic.

It is widely known that the odours of different races vary as much as their colours, but one researcher says there are distinct differences even between complexions. He says that they are 'saucy in brunettes, heady and pervasive as the "nose" of flowery wine in blondes, and sharp and fierce in redheads.' He must have had a whale of a time gathering material for his thesis!

Professional perfumers exploit our convention that natural odours are objectionable and artifical scents, cunningly designed to titillate our senses, are perfectly acceptable. They sell us soap to bring us all to the same level of antiseptic neutrality. Then they sell us expensive musky scents, with glamorous names for the primitive pheromones that Adam and Eve took for granted.

The idea about redheads and foxes may not be so far-fetched after all.

# 37. Partridges on a diet

It gives me great pleasure that from February 2nd until September 1st, it is illegal to shoot a partridge. I am not delighted because I am a spoilsport-Scrooge, hell-bent on denying others every pleasure to which I am not addicted myself. My objection to partridge shooting is far more practical.

Partridges began to decline in numbers about twenty years ago and they are now among our most threatened species. So I would rather see them on a schedule of protected birds than in some trigger-happy fellow's game bag. I know shooting men who are so unimaginative or callous that they still walk up young coveys in September stubble. They would cheerfully blaze away at them till they were extinct on the grounds that, 'If we don't, somebody else would.'

Cartridge manufacturers are not so short-sighted. It is not in their

A red-legged partridge: almost a rarity

interest to wipe out birds that provide a potential market as valuable as if they laid golden eggs. The Eley Game Advisory Service was sired by this acumen. It was an organisation set-up to find alternative markets – or targets – to replace rabbits when myxomatosis struck. Rabbits had accounted for about a million shots a year, but the Game Advisory Service was so successful in showing shooting men how to increase their stocks of game that pheasants are now at the business end of about as much lead shot as rabbits used to be. The Service folded, perhaps because its mission was completed or its title had dropped out of phase with European Conservation Year.

The Game Conservancy now operates from the same headquarters at Fordingbridge in Hampshire. One of the priorities of this conservancy is an investigation of the decline in partridges and the development of management methods to reverse it. The results of the first two years' work confirmed depressing forecasts. Gamekeepers and naturalists have been aware for years that partridges have been growing scarcer. The records in game registers showing the head of game shot on widely dispersed estates, confirm the impression. The cause has been laid at the door of changing methods of farming. Research has already shown that, as with so many generalisations, this is an over-simplification.

I know one keeper who is a real artist with partridges. He has almost managed to keep pace with the declining numbers of his birds by improving his methods of management. He hatches eggs in an incubator and rears intensively. He has discovered that by killing off the old birds at the end of the season, he claims he can double the density of breeding pairs. This has nothing to do with the relative fertility of old and young birds. He believes that an old cock will defend a territory about twice the acreage that a young cock will. Partridges with ambitions for a long life would be wise to emigrate from his beat before their first birthday.

He builds a shelter in each hedge with an ordinary corrugated iron sheet and puts dry sand under it for his birds to get rid of troublesome insect pests by having dustbaths. The hen can settle more contentedly on her eggs if she isn't nagged by bites from itchy fleas and mites. He gets the eggs for his incubator by robbing the early nests. When he has got all he wants, he still takes any small clutches and adds them to the eggs in other nests. The birds so robbed lay another clutch to replace them. So each hen is encouraged to produce twice as many chicks.

The results of research throw an interesting light on the methods my keeper friend has developed by trial and error. In one project, a twenty square mile area was observed and a census taken of the number of resident partridges and chicks reared. A huge vacuum insect net was used to suck the insects off the ground and herbage, enabling an accurate record to be compiled of the insects available for the partridge chicks to eat. It is apparent from this which species of the insect the birds like best and how many they need in order to thrive.

In early life they require about 23 per cent protein in their diet, so a heavy insect crop is vital from early June until July. After that, the older chicks change from insects to a diet of weed seeds and grain. Cold weather in early May makes the crop of aphids, sawflies and other suitable insects late, so the young partridges cannot get enough food to survive after a bad spring.

The fact that my keeper friend steals the first clutches of eggs may actually help the bird to rear her second brood. If she had hatched the first eggs off and it was a cold May, the chicks would not have found enough insects to stave off starvation. But having a second brood much later allows chicks to find enough insects even in a late season. There would also be thicker cover to guard them from crows and cats. Because he hand-rears the chicks hatched in his incubator, he can take care that they get the right amount of protein in their diet.

Perhaps the most interesting thing to emerge from the experiment will be positive methods to encourage insects that are not agricultural pests. If ways of increasing suitable insects can be found, it will not only help partridges but a whole variety of insectivorous birds with no commercial value to sportsmen. It will still be necessary, of course, to convince farmers that any insect is harmless, let alone worth encouraging. But farmers who enjoy shooting or the cash that shooting rents bring, may not be too difficult to convert.

# 38. 'Foxes as big as tigers'

We were walking round the wood after supper the other evening when a fox exploded from a thicket and dashed across the ride ten yards ahead. This was too much for the lurchers who set off in hot pursuit. They are faster than a fox but too intelligent to tangle with his snapping fangs, so I was not unduly worried for their quarry's safety. Five minutes later, they returned with heaving flanks and lolling tongues, vainly trying to fool me that it was only the density of the cover that had saved the fox's brush.

I should have been rather sad if they had done him any mischief, for I don't think the foxes do half as much harm here as the carrion crows and magpies, even to pheasants and partridges. I am fond of our local foxes because they often get me off the hook when I am gazing out of my study window, vainly wondering what to write about. At this critical moment, a fox often seems to cross the ride to distract me. The instant he realises he is exposed to view, his belly and brush merge with the ground till he seems to slither as legless and cunning as a serpent. Yet few animals are more graceful than an unhurried fox, hunting with self-confidence.

This is the best time of year to watch them because the voracious appetite of growing cubs often makes it vital for both dog and vixen to hunt through the hours of daylight.

There is a litter of cubs about half a mile from our house and the vixen is rather small and very red. A real 'foxy' red, as bright as the pictures of my boyhood story books. The dog fox, the chap who excited the lurchers, is very much larger than his vixen, with a coat so dark he looks as if he's been crossed with a silver fox, plucked from the shoulders of some glamorous fashion model.

There is nothing unusual about this, for I know of no other British animal whose coat colour varies so much. It is often as easy to identify individual foxes as shepherds find it to know their sheep or huntsmen their hounds.

I spent some of the best of my childhood rabbiting on the estate of the Vernon family at Hilton outside Wolverhampton. H.V.L. Vernon, the oldest of the four generations I knew, was a methodical man who was exceptionally fond of hunting. I loved to browse through the large glass case in his hall which contained the brushes of between three and four hundred foxes. A macabre ornament with which to delight his guests, you might think, but he was right on target with me.

It taught me the enormous variation in colour of the foxes that had all lived – and died – in this comparatively small area of the Midlands. They did not show just the predictable hues due to the condition of coat or state of moult, but the complete range from white to almost black. And oddly enough 'foxy' red was far from the commonest colour. Most were darker and greyer. This case was also a mine of information about the size of territory which foxes use. Each brush was labelled with the details of how it came to be there. It showed the date of the hunt, where it was found and where it was killed. Any exceptional details were added as a postscript. I have often wondered what happened to those trophies when the estate was finally broken up and Hilton Hall sold. Scientists who are doing research into the habits of foxes would have found the facts amassed in that collection quite invaluable.

If you talk to hunting men about their sport, you will find that they have the same foible as fishermen. They will be full of tales of foxes as big as tigers, which got away; there will be descriptions of unscaleable walls they climbed and unswimable rivers they swam; sagas of the invincible hounds and intrepid huntsmen who so rarely emerged triumphant.

The cold facts in this case filled with fur and labels told a different tale. Although the 'as hounds ran' mileage might have been ten or fifteen, the fact was that few foxes were killed more than three or four miles, as the crow flies, from where they were found. This was called 'a point' of three or four miles. So the scientists would have marked every fox's earth on a large scale map of the area. Then they would have plotted the details of every run from the labels in the case. And, for good measure, they would have dug out the hunting reports from the local papers of the time, plotting the details of where the quarry got away, either by getting safely to ground or when hounds lost his scent.

It would have been a unique method of plotting the factual size of territory which is common among foxes from the routes they had actually taken. My best bet is that, apart from love-lorn dog foxes wandering for miles in winter in search of the dolliest vixens, they would stick to a surprisingly small area. This is because, when they are hunted, they naturally try to get to safety in an area they know well rather than risk landing in strange and possibly inhospitable places.

In support of this theory, I often recognise the same foxes in the same places time after time. It is a natural pattern which is disrupted deliberately when foxhunters go cub-hunting in September. Their object is partly to give young hounds experience of killing foxes and partly to scatter survivors over a wider area than they would naturally choose. The distribution is also altered artificially, especially at this time of year, by those who shoot and gas and snare foxes while they have litters of young cubs.

# 39. Watching the birdwatchers

The behaviour of friends who visit us is as interesting as the animals I spend so much time observing, but even less predictable. Most people like badgers, because badgers are cuddly creatures – or so they think! Ours, having been reared on the bottle, have a fixation for me and probably regard me as a sort of mother-figure-badger. They hold no such illusions about outsiders and one stupid fellow, who pushed his face within inches of the boar badger I was holding, almost lost his nose and caused me to be badly bitten.

The fact is that wild animals do not become domesticated within a generation or so, no matter how tame they are, and I am glad that it is

One of the roe deer feeding with three common geese

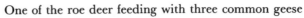

always necessary to treat them with proper respect. Yet, if I mention that, through stupidity, a badger has bitten me, I get a bucketful of letters (that is always where I throw them) complaining because I told the truth, risking badgers being classed as savage beasts and therefore persecuted more.

People who love fox cubs because they have woolly coats and are playful, would change their tune if they picked up a wild cub. Yet, when the cubs have matured into the most lithe and beautiful foxes, the same people will hate them for their cunning and because they catch stupid pheasants.

I am just as illogical myself. Our roe deer gives me special pleasure because roe are notoriously difficult to keep in good health. I was proud when our tame doe had lived a healthy life for eight years, and was still going strong, and that the others demonstrated that they felt at home here by producing young most seasons.

I am always surprised that our friends seem more interested in a trio of common geese, which we simply regard as potential Sunday dinners, than in the roe deer feeding with them. But because geese pose no problems of management, my eyes are introverted to my stomach and fail to convince me that geese are too intelligent and beautiful to end up in the oven.

Three miles from us the reservoir at Blithfield attracts thousands of birds and hundreds of birdwatchers, and I often find the birdwatchers as curious as the birds! Their seasonal gear is as predictable as plumage, and they have just moulted off their open shirts. Chunky anoraks, woolly hats and wellingtons are sprouting in their place. On Sunday mornings, they line the parapet of the bridge across the water, telescopes and powerful binoculars focussed as if they were waiting for the Spanish Armada. When one spots a rarity, a ripple of rising hackles shivers down the line, often to be followed by a squelching mass exodus along the bank to the hide nearest to the object of their curiosity.

Yet few of them are specially interested in the behaviour of the birds they watch. Theirs is more often a collectors' mania and they worship at the altar of rarity. They would rather see a speck on the horizon where something has settled which seldom visits our shores, than watch the whole fascinating life cycle of robins in a nest at home. Some carry check lists of the species it is theoretically possible to see, ticking them off, one by one, like train spotters do with engine numbers.

Although this avian oneupmanship is interesting as an example of human behaviour patterns, its side effects are undoubtedly of benefit to birds. The more people who are interested, even only to the extent of ticking them off on a check list, the greater will be the pressure for their preservation. Those who spend cold, wet nights putting rings on birds' legs in the hope that someone will eventually report where they died or were caught again, are understandably tetchy if they are poisoned with pesticides or netted in thousands for hotel kitchens, when they alight weak from migration on foreign shores.

I confess that I am hooked on a slightly different bait. My appetite is so catholic that I am as fascinated as much by the caterpillars as the birds which eat them. I find as much pleasure in the gorgeous colours of a cock pheasant or common mallard drake, as in some exotic rarity likely to die because it has strayed into our unpredictable climate.

The modern jargon for my addiction is ecology. It may sound pretentious and scientific, but all it really means is studying the relationship between various species and the environment in which they live. It is an extension of the gamekeepers' art, which long ago discovered that pheasants don't mix well with crows and foxes, but do best in woodland which is a mixture of sunny clearings, fringed with berried shrubs, and dense cover surrounded by farm fields.

Naturalists who discovered that tits and redstarts nest in holes, attracted them near enough to observe at close quarters by putting artificial nest boxes in attractive sites. Cotoneaster bushes in your garden may attract rare waxwings on migration and common privet thickets and dense holly bushes will bring you nesting blackbirds whose song will humble nightingales'.

So I enjoy creating conditions where creatures thrive close enough for me to get on intimate terms with them. I don't really mind whether they are rare and difficult, like roe deer, or common and gaudy as starlings. I enjoy the swallows in the garage, even if they do leave no doubt where I park my car, as much as the grasshopper warblers in the wood. And I would rather the wagtails came again to the nest box by the kitchen window than catch a glimpse of some eccentric which came in error.

# 40. Seal a bargain with a spit

A rare delight, in these shifty times, is to discover something much as it was in the past. A stretch of country untrammelled by tarmac; or autumn tints on English oak and beech. There are still some quiet English pubs where the ale comes clear from the wood – if you know where to find them. And the smell of wood smoke and home-cured bacon still drifts from cottage chimneys.

I suppose that horsey folk have changed as little as most, though I have a theory that too many hours in the saddle can shake their brains down into their breeches.

A chap from Bloxwich was inordinately proud of his pair of matching carriage horses till one of them went sick. So he decided to cut his losses, sell it at Rugeley horse fair, and buy another as like it as he could. In those days, horses were not sold under the hammer by auctioneer, but bargained for in the street. Dealers gathered with their strings of horses, tied them up and sat by them as patiently as spiders in their webs, as they still do in the wilder parts of Ireland.

When the chap with the ailing horse arrived, a dealer came up and pointed out not only the fault that had caused him to decide to sell, but a nap hand of blemishes besides. He almost convinced him that he would be doing him a good turn if he took the old screw off his hands as a gift. So the owner was delighted to accept a pound or two and the promise that the man would soon be back with the perfect replacement.

The next few hours passed pleasantly enough in the Shrewsbury Arms till the dealer turned up with a gleaming, spirited horse. It was an almost perfect match for the one he'd left at home. Although it cost him much more than he'd bargained for, he returned in triumph. But his groom took one look and said, "But you've brought your own horse back, sir!" He took the bridle off and the old nag walked straight into the stall where he'd stood for years!

There are more tricks in horse dealing than fleas on a hedgehog. A lump of ginger under his tail had 'gingered him up'. A dab or two of dye and a bit of skilful tittivating had produced such a transformation that even his owner did not recognise him.

There are no more horse fairs at Rugeley now, for the stench of hot engine oil is commoner in the country than the friendly smell of horses. Streets no longer crackle with sparks kicked off the cobbles by iron horse shoes.

One of the few such fairs to survive is at Stow-on-theWold in the Cotswolds. In 1476, the Abbot of Evesham was granted a charter to hold one fair there in May, and one in October. One celebrates the feast of St Philip and St James, and the other the Translation of King Edward the Confessor to the Company of Saints.

In the old days, crowds converged on Stow-on-the-Wold, 'where the wind blows cold' from all over England. For almost five centuries they rode or drove their horses there, often taking weeks to travel down the pack-horse roads of Wales or along the Pennines or from London, dealing at other fairs on the way. They don't ride their horses there now, of course, but bring them in horse boxes and cattle trucks. And the buyers and spectators fill a field with cars.

When I was there for the October fair, they didn't impress me as being particularly saintly. They were the same brash, horsey, colourful crowd that had congregated there since you could count the centuries on the fingers of one hand.

An auctioneer was perched on a straw bale rostrum in a field above the town, exposed to the coldest winds that blow on the wolds. He intoned incessant bids over a loudspeaker that had probably relayed pop at the village hop the night before. This was all highly respectable, and impeccable hunters from fashionable packs changed hands for hundreds of guineas. They were selling carriages and traps and harness and saddles and racing sulkies in another ring.

But in the road outside was a horse fair of an older kind. An unofficial horse fair where sellers didn't have to worry so much about warranties and auctioneers' commission and such modern conventions. They haggled and bargained as their ancestors had done down the centuries. They tied their horses up by the roadside, apparently indifferent whether they sold them or not.

Some were gypsies with lurcher dogs as capable of filling the pot with poached rabbits and hares as ever their ancestors were. Their women were brown-eyed and attractive enough to charm dowries out of misers.

The buyers were other gypsies and scrap-tatters, or respectable mums out to get a cheap pony for the kids. Horsey men looked for bargains, and folk like me just went for a day out to watch the eternal drama of fortunes made and lost. The dealing was done at the leisurely pace of an eastern market. When the price approached reality, they put a lad on the horse and sent him careering through the crowds and traffic to show off its paces. One of these hair-raising charges nearly floored a policeman but nobody seemed to care.

When a deal was done, the cash was winkled out of secret pockets and counted note by note. Then the seller solemnly spat on the last greasy piece of paper and returned it to the buyer as 'luck money'. Such old ways sometimes seem more civilised than modern legal contracts.

# 41. The real Tiggy - Winkles

I can count on the fingers of one hand the number of times I have been to the cinema in the last twenty years. Although I have usually been disappointed, I found *The Tales of Beatrix Potter* an exception.

It is so long since I read her books that I had not realised how deeply they must have affected me. Her tales had penetrated the murk of my Black Country childhood to weave into my mind an immutable affection for the characters she painted. Perhaps I should have taken far less subsequent trouble to get to know real badgers if I had not been reared on the saga of Mr Tod. I loved her Squirrel Nutkin. And no rabbit ever did wrong in my eyes after I had been introduced to Peter Rabbit and Benjamin Bunny.

The film winkled a magnum of memories out of my subconscious mind which seemed to focus on Mrs Tiggy-Winkle. She was a hedgehog, and so was the first wild animal I ever tamed.

Tick investigating a prickly ball

I was about eight at the time and I had been given permission to catch the rabbits on Bloxwich golf course. I had ferrets, nets, a good terrier, and would have backed myself as more than a match for most modern pest officers. I didn't just go ferreting. I went out at first light of dewy dawn and followed dusk into darkness in the evenings.

Mick, my old mongrel bull terrier, often found hedgehogs – urchins we always called them – and sat by them until I retraced my steps to see what had happened to him. I took one of these urchins home and shut it in a fowl pen and fed it on bread and milk until it was tame. It was one of the most attractive pets I ever had. *The Tales of Beatrix Potter* took me back to those days. The only character they lacked was my old Mick.

Years later, after I was married, hedgehogs crossed my path again. A distinguished professor of bacteriology asked a friend of mine to get hedgehogs for his research. My friend, who lived in Hampshire, had a wry sense of humour and replied that he could easily catch all the hedgehogs he wanted. The only snag was that the railway, he said, was so slow that they would probably die before they reached their destination. He said it would be wiser to get them locally and gave my address as a certain supplier.

The result was that I received a letter requesting me to produce twelve hedgehogs and deliver them to the University of Birmingham. Pipe dreams of mythical feats of my childhood convinced me that the challenge was a pushover. My only worry was that I have an instinctive revulsion to vivisection and could not tolerate the thought of 'my' hedgehogs suffering under the scalpel of some itchy-fingered scientist. The professor reassured me. All he wanted to do was to feed the hedgehogs some parisite-infected meat and to see if their digestion sterilised the bacteria or if it might be transmitted by their dropping to another farm. When he had satisfied himself one way or the other, he promised to return them to the wild. But I soon regretted my optimism in rating it an easy task to catch that dozen.

I have often wondered since if *The Tales of Beatrix Potter* were originally responsible for the interest so many scientists have lavished on hedgehogs. They have discovered that, though their brains are too small for great intelligence, their powers of scent are exceptional. They have dissected their prickles to show that they are specially adapted strands of hair, so formed that they stand erect if the animal is alarmed and tautens its skin. They are pointed at one end so that they serve the double purpose of a weapon of defence and an effective shock absorber if the creature falls when climbing.

The scientists will assure you that hibernation is accompanied by a migration of white blood corpuscles from the blood to a mass which coats the stomach and the bowel. This is because the whole process of living slows down in hibernation to a point where there could be little resistance to bacterial infection. So Nature concentrates the white corpuscles where their defence is likely to be most effective.

Some scientists – and I would hate a hedgehog to fall into their hands through any fault of mine – have done research into temperature changes during hibernation. They have planted one thermometer just beneath the skin and another more delicate recording instrument on a needle inside the heart. They have discovered that the skin falls to whatever the temperature of the air around reaches but that the heart and centre of the body remain very constant. Then they have plotted the temperature gradient on a graph. Sticking needles into hedgehogs' hearts seems to me an extortionate price to pay for such academic knowledge. Other scientists have proved that the respiration rate in winter sometimes falls as low as a breath in four or five minutes, and the sugar in the blood sinks to half its summer value. Such research may be rewarding to the scientists, but I get more kicks from rescuing hedgehogs than from pinning them on to dissecting boards.

Coming home late the other night, I surprised my passengers by suddenly pulling up in an apparently empty country lane. If I hadn't, I should have run over a hedgehog. I saw the car in front of me miss him by inches and I assessed the odds against his survival as pretty high.

So I got out and picked him up and put him in the boot. Now he has settled down in our garden and wood where he will be safe from scientists and motor cars alike. I think Beatrix Potter would have approved.

# 42. Free harvest

My ancient aunt was pretty strait-laced. She equated gin with sin. So I am sure she would have disapproved my motives the other afternoon when I spent a pleasant hour or so picking sloes. My pleasure was in anticipation. I should be able to make sloe gin for Christmas which my friends and I prefer to more conventional expensive liqueurs.

It is easy enough to make. A pound of sloes are punctured with a fine fork or darning needle and put in a jar with a pound of lump sugar and a bottle of gin. The mixture is shaken daily for a fortnight and then strained into bottles – not to be taken before Christmas! By that time, the spirit has been fortified and the sloes have endowed the viscid fluid with a mellow flavour as good as the best liqueurs – for the price of a bottle of gin. Although it is relatively cheap to make in terms of hard cash, the price is pretty high if you take personal discomfort into account.

Sloes are really wild damsons that grow on blackthorn hedges and, as every countryman knows, the spikes on blackthorn are as bad as the most vicious barbed wire. My hands and wrists got so lacerated that I would have preferred a Far Eastern fakir's bed of nails. I had to project my mind to the heady delights of the future in order to discipline myself to endure the torture of the prickly present.

Blackthorn is such an early flower than it often blooms in frost and snow before less foolish trees have burst their buds. So it is not surprising that it suffers from frigidity and has no chance to fruit in seasons when it chooses too cold a spell to blossom. This year, the blackthorn bushes stood out in purple patches of bellyaching fruit. Raw sloes are bitter as gall so that I marvel at the inspiration of the genius who first had faith to risk contaminating good gin with sloes and sugar.

Our wood is predominantly oak and silver birch and, before we came, I had never bothered to think much about oak trees, but took it for granted that they were all the same. Now I find that there are four or five varieties in our wood and they all seem to behave differently. Some have been bare of leaves for weeks and their branches are silhouetted against the sky. Others are as deep green now as they were in July and show no sign of surrendering to the season. Between these extremes are trees of every subtle shade from delicate greeny-fawn to rich russet.

As the pale sun shone on them the other afternoon, I thought that autumn was the loveliest time of the year and England the most perfect place on earth. The gaudy splendour of the most flashy foreign land is tawdry by comparison. The hedge where I was picking my sloes at the edge of the wood had not rationed itself to the purple bounty of the fruit I sought. There were drifts of crimson hawthorn berries, which would later feed a flock of birds, interspersed with scarlet hips that had started life as demure wild roses.

The charm of the English countryside at any season is that it is never static. The most brilliant artist, I feel, cannot capture it with his dead daubs on canvas. It is the scudding white clouds against the blue skies that give it life, or strutting cock pheasants or mallard drakes floating on a leaden pool.

On the other side of my hedge a bright red tractor was ploughing a corn stubble because the moment the soil has yielded one harvest it must be groomed into condition for the next. A swirling cloud of sea-gulls weaved intricate designs. They were waiting to swoop on worms exposed as the plough share turned fresh earth over into the light. When I was a child, seagulls inland and aeroplanes were both such rarities that we rushed outdoors to see them. Now both are common, but both still seem out of place to me and I am not resigned to either.

When I had gathered all the sloes I needed, I wandered through the wood down to the pool by the house. It is one of the most peaceful spots I know and the wind usually drops to a whisper at dusk so that the surface of the water is as still as a mirror. Or it would be if it were not for the wild duck there.

At about sunset, the duck which have been preening their plumage for the last hour or so on the bank, decide it is time for their nightly forage. They come down to the water's edge in twos and threes, to drink and bathe and they fill the quiet air with the sudden babble of their conversation. When the sun sinks low enough to light the surface of the water with its horizontal beams, the duck take flight. They don't dash off greedily to feed on fallen grain on local stubbles or acorns in the wood. They fly round a while, repeatedly returning to the water they love so much. They take sensual delight in landing fast enough to spurt up bow waves before them, and repeat the manoeuvres at ever-changing angles. The patterns they weave in the sunset on the still surface of the water are among the most beautiful sights of the country-side.

I stayed watching them till the light faded and then the dogs and I settled by a roaring log fire to prepare my sloes for Christmas.

# 43. All steamed-up

Bloodsports are an emotive topic which have caused arguments of varying shades of rancour for generations. There are three quite different reasons for disliking them. The first and most obvious is that they are cruel. The second is that the pursuit of the quarry may have a serious effect on the survival of its species. The third is that people enjoy them.

Otters are declining for a number of reasons. Modern methods of drainage have resulted in the trees along the banks of rivers being felled, which has removed many holts that otters slept and bred in. And the increasing pressure of people using river banks for leisure has also had an effect. The population of otters seems to have been fairly static for a century before the last war, so it is doubtful if hunting alone would have had a serious effect on their numbers. Added to their other perils, though, it could well be the last straw so that there is a very strong argument for banning otter-hunting solely on the grounds that the species needs protection.

Foxes are not under the same threat because increasing areas of afforestration and the fact that they have adapted reasonably well to urban life ensures that their numbers are in no immediate danger.

It may be significant that the majority of opponents of bloodsports are townsfolk; many people brought up in the country accept hunting as a normal part of rural life. If you hatch, rear and feed your own chickens, then kill them and dress them personally, you are more likely to take their sudden death for granted than if your only contact with poultry is a pre-packed oven-ready chicken from a supermarket.

Before condemning foxhunting simply on the grounds of cruelty, it is not unreasonable to compare it objectively with the probable alternatives, however unpleasant they may seem. I imagine I have seen as many foxes die as most of my readers. Once, and only once, I am glad to say, I saw a fox caught by the foot in a gin trap, which is now mercifully illegal. It appeared simply horrific, but I doubt if even that was as bad as it seemed. When I was a boy, I once caught my thumb in a 4 inch rabbit gin. The grip was so fierce that I felt no pain at the time because numbness set in almost instantaneously. It did not start to throb for about an hour after release, and then I suffered several sleepless nights.

Hanging foxes in wire snares is probably the commonest and most effective way of catching them. An extraordinary facet of their nature is that they make regular 'runs' through gaps in hedges or fences, and once they start to use them, they go on the same way night after night, generation after generation. This is obvious to any observant eye because they leave a well-worn track as clear as a footpath across a grass field.

I know lots of countrymen who are skilled at setting a snare in one of these runs so that the next fox to pass puts his head in the noose which tightens round his neck. It is by no means uncommon to catch twenty or thirty foxes in the same hang in the same run in the same season. Rabbits or hares so caught bumble around in blind panic until the noose tightens and strangles them. Foxes are not so stupid. They try to escape but ease off before their struggles are fatal. Then they get the worst of both worlds by waiting in terror till the man who laid the trap comes round to put them out of their misery. Modern 'self-lock' snares, which are supposed to avoid this, are far worse if the wire tightens anywhere but round the neck. Some people poison foxes, which has the disadvantage of being dangerously unselective as well as illegal. I am particularly bitter about this because my favourite bitch picked up poison laid, I believe, by someone for vermin.

In spring, it is sometimes possible to gas foxes when they are still underground with their cubs, though where cover is thick enough some foxes stay above ground all the year round. The objection to this method is that it is also unselective, though cyanide poisoning is relatively swift and humane. But foxes often use the same earths as badgers and it is illegal, and unpardonable, to gas badgers, which are under great pressure at the moment. In spite of the 1975 Badgers Act protecting them, gangs still dig them out with terriers to sell their cubs illegally as pets, and their skins for way-out gear.

I have operated a cage trap for many years, but adult foxes soon grow trap-shy so that it is only really effective in exceptionally hard weather or when vixens grow bold while feeding cubs.

The last common alternative to hunting is shooting, which has little that commends it to me. The farmers who organise fox shoots may be excellent shots, but it is difficult to persuade them to hold their fire except at lethal range. They tend to let go at anything in sight because foxes are supposed to be slow healers and infect their own wounds by licking them immediately after eating carrion. Countrymen believe that if they hit a fox, it will die – eventually.

Only fools claim that foxes enjoy being hunted, despite the fact that there are plenty of authenticated instances of foxes killing fowl or ducks when hounds are not far behind. All that this implies is that foxes are not imaginative enough to visualise terror in the abstract. I have no doubt that they find it very unpleasant when hounds get within striking distance but they would reckon their end was equally cruel if they were shot or trapped or snared instead.

But, however one regards it, there is no doubt that hunting is a perfectly legal sport until a law is passed to ban it. The worst of all reasons for opposing it is that other people enjoy it. What people enjoy is their own affair, and it is stupid to cloud the issue with emotional arguments about abirtary matters of taste.

# 44. Accountants in the tractor saddle

I sometimes think that my favourite time of the year is each season as it passes. The tender greens of English spring are sweeter than the grass anywhere else in the world at any other time. The gentle warmth of English summer is so much kinder than foreign suns which toast tender skins a withered brown and highlight the jaundiced eyes of whisky-swigging colonists. Our frosts are sharp but not cruel and English snows are picturesque but rarely lie long enough to wear their welcome out. This is the moment when I am convinced that nowhere else is as satisfying and mellow as an English autumn.

Stubble-burning: is this an awful waste?

There are a thousand acres of stubble to the north-east of our wood. Here is a golden status symbol of the success of the farmers who have crammed their barns with golden riches of grain. This success started several years ago. First they planned the rotation of crops to follow uncounted years of lying fallow under Needwood Forest and the parkland which stretched to our boundary. Potatoes and beans and sheep and cattle took turns in grooming the ground for its present fertility. The seed went in last autumn, sprouted and grew in spring. Then it was cossetted and fertilised and sprayed until the combine harvesters grazed their way though it about three weeks ago. By the time this wealth had been safely banked in the granary, the stubble bristled with the pride of a bemedalled colonel, respectably barbered with short-back-and sides.

We're lucky where I live. There is not so much corn as grass because the Uttoxeter district is famous for its cattle. So straw is at a premium. Cattle yards are strawed down deep in winter to provide muck to swell the crops the next year. Cattle need warm bedding so that food goes into flesh and milk instead of being wasted as an expensive form of central heating.

Every Wednesday, dealers roll up at the cattle auction with trucks piled high with straw. They barter it for beasts so that everyone goes home as satisfied as successful traders in olden times. Cornfields around here are neat and prosperous. When both corn and straw have been harvested and the stubble stripped of its riches, the brown soil is left to weather ready for next year's crop.

Last week I spent a day in the eastern counties where things were sadly different. They grow more corn but have fewer cattle than we do. Most seasons, they don't need the straw and transport costs rule out any idea of carting it far to sell. If they left it on the stubble it would clog the plough – so they set it alight. I couldn't help feeling pity for the mice and voles and frogs and insects in the path of the fires. Even small birds panicked in the smoke because they didn't know in which direction safety lay. They suffered the choking fog of fumes, a spasm of agonising hellish heat – and then were sacrificed on the altar of easy money.

The farmers of those corn-growing counties are not different from the chaps who are my neighbours. They are not vandals, addicted to arson for the kicks of seeing a few mice fry, so why do they operate their scorched earth policy?

Perhaps some of them formulate policy but never get near enough the ground to get muck on their boots. They operate the theory that what pays is right. When that sort get big enough, with enough capital locked-up in mechanisation and land, they cease to calculate their profits in pounds per acre. They think, instead, in terms of return on capital invested. Somehow, hard cash is far less personal than fertile soil crumbling through loving fingers.

A cow that knows your voice, the daughter and grand-daughter of beasts you bred, is more than mere figures in a ledger. But if her milk production falls below average, she will mean no more to the clerk who signs her death sentence than scratching out his records. Her chances would be infinitely better with the chap who coaxed the first milk out of her as a heifer, acted as midwife each year after and became personally involved. His soul would be dead if he could feel no pang at parting when the butcher called.

To real farmers, the same applies to crops. They love their land, and scheme and calculate how to harvest the crops without stealing the fertility. They walk every acre, hating the weeds like enemies, gambling on quirks of weather, when to sow and when to reap. They suffer frost and wet and heat and fatigue, and enjoy the sensual thrill of handling the fruits of the plenty they create. So firing stubble and wasting straw, which could comfort cattle and manure crops, goes against the grain. They do it only for the reason that they cannot afford to do otherwise. They cannot afford the wages for the traditional husbandry of their ancestors. Our affluent society is pricing men out of the market so that they become redundant while machines take over. Machines will do in hours what it took a man weeks to do by hand. We have reached the stage that, when a job is uneconomic by machine, we have convinced ourselves that it is not worth doing at all. So, in areas where the demand for straw bedding is low, it is cheaper to burn the stubble than to harvest it.

This may be progress in accountants' minds, but it seems a crazy world to me.

# 45. The goose is a 'fulish' bird

Urban friends are often surprised that we can eat the poultry that we have reared to maturity. They imply that we must be utterly callous or devoid of imagination to enjoy the flesh of what would have become pets to them. It reminds them of the boy who wanted to be a butcher because he was fond of animals. I suppose that the answer is that country folk have practical and earthy minds. Cattle and pigs and sheep have been tended with loving care since Time was young and yet their husbandmen have never flinched from taking them as a crop when ripe.

However illogical it may seem, I shudder at the practices of modern factory farming and would have no part in them. The stench of pigs kept in sweat boxes or eating food off the floor where they have dunged, so sickens me that the thought of them on a plate would turn me up. I hate to see battery hens crammed three to a cage with their food passing them on one conveyor belt at the side and their droppings removed by another below. It devalues their dignity to use them as machines. What ever the protagonists of such intensive husbandry may say about their lives being made happy by ideally controlled environments, it seems to me such an unnatural life that I do not concede its justification.

Such birds often look pale and liverish and react to scientific stimulus so predictably that they wear themselves out in a season. There is nothing to be got out of life that isn't put in, so I prefer to eat eggs from my own birds that have been reared on fresh green grass and scratched for insects on free range. They may not be so commercially viable, but at least they have a happy and natural life while it lasts, so I have no compunction about eating their flesh as well as their eggs in return.

Geese were among the first birds to be domesticated by man, though not originally for his table. A Greylag was probably the daddy of them all. Yet in spite of being such shy birds, they are unusually easy to tame. This is because of the way in which young geese become 'imprinted'. When they hatch from the eggs, they have an instinctive urge to follow whatever they see move first, and they go on regarding it as their parent. Normally this is fine because the first creature they are likely to see is the female goose that hatched them. The fact that their impulse is to follow her wherever she goes is all to the good. But if a man happens to approach a goose's nest while the eggs are hatching, the young goslings may regard him henceforth as Mum.

It is believed that this happened in primitive times, so ancient civilisations often kept domesticated geese. They did not initially have them for food, and they were kept by the priests in Egypt five thousand years ago as part of their religion. Perhaps the Egyptians marvelled that such wild birds regarded them as friends because Man's deep psychological craving is for affection. Perhaps the priests tamed them to show their followers, who had never heard of 'imprinting', how clever they were, weaving the geese into the pattern of all sorts of religious beliefs.

The golden egg in the fairy tale started off as the sun in pagan religion because primitive people believed that the sun was laid in the sky when a skein of geese flew by. "On Candlemas Day, all good geese should lay." "When winter is dying and the old goose laying, it means that spring is not far behind" – however much February weather shakes your faith in such ideas. When Julius Caesar came to Britain, he found that the ancient Britons kept geese but did not eat them because they were sacred birds.

Gradually religion degenerated into folklore so that geese whose ancestors had been reverenced and worshipped were used for sacrifice and became the focal point of feasts. It became traditional to gorge on fat goose at Michaelmas and Martinmas, the feasts of St Michael and St Martin. So the priests who first discovered geese were good for food as well as worship were thoroughly practical chaps.

I'm glad they were. I know of no smell so sweet as fat goose cooking in the oven; no taste as good as when it comes out sizzling. An old Black Country saying proclaims that a goose is a very 'fulish' – (or foolish) – bird; too big for one, not big enough for two. The heavy industry in the Black Country gave men prodigious appetites!

I also associate roast goose particularly with Staffordshire because of a ceremony which was once performed at Hilton, near Wolverhampton. The Lord of the Manor of Essington owed allegiance to the neighbouring Lord of Hilton. The conditions under which his estate was held stipulated that he must go to Hilton with a live goose on New Year's Eve.

At Hilton in the Middle Ages a hollow bronze figure called Jack of Hilton was filled with water and put close to the fire, which in those days was in the centre of the great hall. Jack was naked, ugly and, even by our modern permissive standards, exceedingly virile and rude. The heat of the fire boiled the water inside him so rapidly that it spurted out as a fierce jet of dry steam which added fury to the flames.

While Jack was acting as a pair of bellows, my Lord of Essington had to drive his goose three times round the fire. It was then taken away to be killed and cooked while he and his host put in a spell of hard drinking. When the ceremony finished, my Lord of Essington acknowledged his Lord of Hilton's superiority by serving him with a dish of the roast goose. Then they polished off the bird between them. I wish I had been there to join them.

# 46. The graceful predator

Stoats have few friends in the countryside, even among other stoats. Keepers try to trap them before they have time to decimate their pheasants. Farmers try to shoot them before they raid their fowl pens, and sportsmen measure their terriers' worth by the number of stoats they have killed.

When two strange dog stoats meet, they will fight for a mate or a meal with spontaneous dedication. Even as lovers, stoats have carved a special niche for themselves in folklore. The bitch stoat plays hard-to-get and the dog stoat pursues her relentlessly until sheer exhaustion forces her submission. His ardour in conquest is so notorious that a man with a similar one-track mind is classed by society as 'a bit of a stoat'.

My friendly female stoat

Of all the wild creatures which roam the countryside, they are probably the fiercest and most bloodthirsty for their size. But, as so often happens with those who get a bad name, they are not as black as they are painted. On balance, most predators do more good than harm, provided their numbers do not swell out of proportion. Before the days of myxomatosis, when rabbits were a real plague, stoats were their most effective control.

I've often watched a stoat hunting a rabbit and thought that he'd forgotten more about scent than the cleverest master of fox hounds will ever know. He can single out a victim and stick to it faultlessly. When the rabbit has tried to throw him off the scent, I have watched him puzzle out every twist and quirk as accurately as the finest bloodhound with the most sensitive nose. If his quarry bolts down a hole, the stoat will pursue it until it pops out again as sharp as a champagne cork. If it dives into thick cover, he follows its gyrations as persistently as a shadow.

Most brilliant of all, he can stick to the scent of his chosen rabbit even if it rushes deliberately through a whole horde of other rabbits. This is the acid test of all huntsmen and, in the days when newspapers regularly reported the runs of foxhounds in their area, the commonest cause of a blank day was claimed to be that they had changed onto a fresh scent.

When the hunted fox was tiring, he was often wily enough to find a fresh one and lie down beside it. When this heard the hounds approaching, it would rush off in a panic to get as far away as possible and hounds followed it without realising they had lost their beaten fox. Clever huntsmen are always on the lookout for this and, if they catch a glimpse of a fresh fox in front of hounds, they will stop them and cast back to find their original pilot.

Stoats need no such human aid. A stoat knows which rabbit it is chasing by its individual scent – and the fascinating thing is that other rabbits know that it knows! I have seen scores grazing in the open when a single rabbit has gone right through the crowd, closely pursued by a stoat. Expecting them to scatter in all directions, I am always astonished to see them move aside only a few yards with no sign of panic. As soon as the stoat and the rabbit he is hunting have passed, the others resume feeding fatalistically confident that there is no point in worrying until they are selected for the hunt.

Equally obviously, the victim knows his doom is certain and, long before the stoat catches him in fair chase, he throws in the sponge, squats down and squeals blue murder. The stoat comes up, leaps upon his back and kills him with a bite at the base of the skull.

Generations of countrymen have watched this drama and, being practical fellows, they have chivvied the victor off and pinched his spoils to make rabbit pie. When I once did so, the stoat only retired a few paces to the safety of a hollow stump from which he chattered and spat at me in impotent rage for using my size so unfairly.

The more you know about such ferocious beasts, the more impossible it seems to tame one, but I have long had my doubts. I had two perfectly delightful tame weasels about twenty years ago. They have a great deal in common with stoats. They look very alike, the main difference being that a stoat is larger than a weasel and he has a black tip to his tail. In cold climates, stoats turn white in winter, when their fur is known as ermine. Only the tip of the tail remains black and it is this which forms the black tippets in the robes of mayors and such other dignitaries as enjoy dressing up.

My weasels were chocolate brown on top with snowy white waistcoats. They were playful, affectionate and thoroughly delightful. Since then, I have always longed to try my hand at striking up a friendship with a stoat but I have had to wait until this summer.

A few weeks ago, a gamekeeper saw a bitch stoat scurrying across a track carrying a youngster by the scruff of the neck. He had not got his gun, so he shouted and gave chase. The old stoat dropped her burden and escaped to the safety of thick cover from where she chattered her abuse.

The keeper picked up the tiny stoat kitten and took it home to show the family. His wife was enchanted by it and reared it, first on milk and then on dead birds and rabbits. The snag was that the nicest tame stoat might forget her manners if she escaped to the pheasant pens. So they took extraordinary precautions for security.

When I first saw her, she was sleeping between the pillows on the keeper's double bed so that, if she did escape from the bedroom, she still had to breach the defences downstairs before she could do any damage. Such confinement has obvious disadvantages, however fond you are of stoats. So she came to me.

The most playful kitten is a clumsy lout compared to her. She whizzes round my study as gracefully as leaves spinning in the wind and it is impossible to predict where she will turn up in the next fraction of a second. She is also surprisingly vocal, and when she is playing, she emits a high-pitched purr as she croons the tune of her content. As with beautiful females of our own species, she is not slow to say so if she's crossed. When I give her food, for instance, she purrs in one breath and chatters and hisses defiance with the next – suspicious that I may want to share it.

I have already had great fun making tape recordings of her vocabulary and comparing them to records of my old tame badger and weasel. The language of all three has marked similarities which emphasize how right the old naturalists were who lumped them all under the same latin family name of mustilidae.

When she has done playing and crooning, spitting and hissing, she pops down the neck of my shirt and curls up to take a nap. She is as lithe and elegant in repose as in the explosion of her play. If she does escape, I shall no more grudge her an exotic pheasant than I would grudge a box of chocolates to a girl not half so pretty.

# Winter

# 47. Cure for a hangover

Thick heads after Christmas were once as common as berries on a hawthorn tree. Countrymen were suspicious of new-fangled dishes and vintage wines. They regarded sophisticated continental cooking as mucking good food around, and made no bones about their preference for the simple things of life. But consuming vast quantities of home-fed roast goose washed down by quarts of honest English ale, produced results just as painful as Christmassing too well on more exotic fare.

Rural cures for such basic complaints owed nothing to antibiotics. Why bother the doctor when a few hours ferreting on Boxing Day had far more therapeutic effect than a gallon of his physic? Rabbiting with ferrets and guns used to be the traditional way of ending Christmas in the country.

I was never much for shooting. Unkind friends said that I couldn't hit the parish I was born in. I always preferred to work with a ferret and

Tick and a ferret

nets. My pointer, Tick, positively wriggles with delight when she sees me get out a ferret, her mind and mine are so closely in tune.

I have owned a more or less constant succession of ferrets since I was nine years old and I soon learned that the secret of successful ferretting was stealthy silence. If rabbits knew there were men or dogs about, they stayed stubbornly below ground. The ferret often killed them, gorged on the spoils of victory – then curled up to sleep it off. This could mean long hours of waiting, shrivelled by bitter biting winds, hoping against hope that the ferret would show up. The more constructive remedy was to put a 'liner' down. This was a hob ferret, a male as large and strong as possible, who was kept in a hutch by himself. It was vital that he met a loose ferret as a stranger and not as an old friend who might be willing to share the feast and curl up with him!

The liner was fitted with a small leather collar attached to a line of cord about ten yards long. The cord had a knot every yard and, as the ferret went below ground, the chap who was working him – usually me – counted the knots as they disappeared. The ferret stopped when he reached the rabbit and an arc was traced off the surface of the ground of three or four or five yards radius, depending on how many yards had been paid out.

The next thing was to lie flat on the ground, above the spot where he might be, in the hopes of hearing a scuffle. That was the signal for the men with spades to dig down to try to open the subterranean tunnels and expose the errant ferrets with their booty. I have seen strong man strain at this unpaid toil till the frosty air was steamy with their sweat. If the price of their labour had been totted-up as wages, rabbits would have cost more than caviar. But they counted it as sport and were rewarded for their efforts with the quickest cure for a Christams hang-over that was ever devised!

I always regarded the necessity to dig out a ferret as a slur on my expertise. When I was silent and skilful enough, the sport was often fast and furious though it was not always the rabbits that were in peril.

One Boxing Day I was crouching on all fours in a hedge bottom, paying out the ferret line through sensitive fingers. A rabbit suddenly bobbed up and sat within arm's reach of the mouth of his hole, surveying his chances of escape. I froze into immobility, lest I scare him back. The golden rule for all men with guns is never to fire till there is nothing in the background but the quarry. Resisting such temptation did not appear to be among the virtues of the chap standing about twenty yards out in the field behind me. He took careful aim at his sitting target, missed it clean – and blew a hole in the hedge a foot from my head!

Although Boxing Day wouldn't have seemed right without a few hours rabbiting, I was really far keener on ratting. For years, I kept Stafford bull terriers, descended from the old fighting dogs of the Black Country, for no breed on earth can touch them for ratting.

Years ago, when I worked in a factory in West Bromwich, I got married and went to live in a flat above a shop in the high street. My bull terrier, Grip, naturally came with us but, long suffering as she has always been, my wife did jib at ferrets in the flat. I have never been one to take No as an answer, so I persuaded the boss to let me use the bedroom of a cottage in the works till it was demolished to make room for a workshop. My ferrets were reprieved and I was able to spend my free mornings with them while the Sunday dinner was being cooked at home.

It was a sport that has always appealed to lads so that I usually had a disciple learning some of the things he should know – and some he shouldn't. We'd caught a lot of rats one day and the lad persuaded me to let him pop a live young one, a bit bigger than a mouse, into his pocket. He wanted to take it home and bring it up tame as a pet. Few party tricks are more arresting that the surprise appearance of a large and apparently wild rat! The lad, who has since graduated as a highly respected auctioneer, came home to lunch. My wife, whose ideas of what such lads should learn do not always tally with mine, later took him on a tour of some of the places he should see. They were halfway up the aisle of Tong church, admiring the superbly sculptured tombs, when young Mac blurted out in a hoarse stage whisper, "Mrs Drabble, Mrs Drabble – *my rat!!*"

Till then it had skulked in the friendly cover of his pocket, but suddenly decided to pop out and was running down the aisle in front of them. They both made valiant but ineffective efforts to recapture it until it eventually dodged past them down the grating over the central heating. So they pretended it had nothing to do with them and sneaked away, wondering what effect it would have on the preacher if it decided to emerge and listen to the sermon.

# 48. Big-hearted midgets

A pleasant facet of my life is that the clock is not my master. My routine is geared more to the hours of daylight than to the pips on the wireless, so when nights draw-in I take the dogs into the woods and feed the stock early in the afternoon. By the time the pheasants have fed and flown safely up to roost at dusk, the dogs have settled on the hearthrug in front of a roaring fire.

We never draw the curtains till darkness falls and, the other night, we were watching the patterns on the pool made by the wild duck flying to and from their feeding grounds at sunset.

Our attention was suddenly distracted by a party of wrens flying into the honeysuckle which clothes the gable end. First one flew up and then another and another until twelve tiny birds has disappeared under the eaves.

A Jenny wren – as she is known in the country – is a warm brown little bird, often seen creeping about in thick cover, searching for spiders and small insects. She seems as agile as a fox terrier hunting for rabbits in a bramble bush. Her chattering voice is arrogant in anger but, when his temper is sweet, her mate pours out songs of love loud enough to come from the heart of a lion.

The recent series of mild winters suited wrens which are now quite common, even in suburban gardens. They were so rare that people feared for their survival after the cruel winter of 1963. It almost wiped them out. Prolonged icy spells are obviously dangerous to insectivorous birds. The cold kills the creatures they feed on or buries them under an impenetrable blanket of snow.

Birds as small as wrens are subject to an even worse peril than slow starvation. The surface area of their bodies is so large in proportion to their volume it is almost impossible for a single bird to retain enough body heat to sustain life throughout a bitter winter's night. In really hard weather, wrens are more likely to dissipate their vital warmth by radiation at night than to die of starvation by day.

They have evolved a wonderful way of cheating death by combining to fight their common foe. Quite large numbers settle together and sleep in a communal roost to keep each other warm. When I saw so many wrens disappearing into our honeysuckle, I knew that they must have found a suitable spot for a communal roost somewhere under our eaves.

I didn't dare risk disturbing them by looking for them by flashlight so I noted the time precisely and settled by the window ten minutes earlier the next evening. Nearly all wild birds and animals are slaves of habit and I was pretty sure that I shouldn't have long to wait because the odds were that they would be punctual. Within seconds, a wren perched on the iron wicket gate into the garden and burst into a loud song as if he was playing 'Lights Out'. The rest of the squad fell-in and all twelve disappeared into an open fronted nest box where a pair of robins reared their brood last year.

Next morning, I took down the box and cut a hole in the side the exact size to allow the business end of a microphone to project into the box. I also poked in the tip of a sensitive electronic thermometer to try to discover just how much a living ball of such tiny birds raised the temperature in their sleeping quarters.

Neither experiment was very successful. I wired the microphone to my tape recorder but discovered that flocks of jackdaws flew over to roost in the wood at the precise time 'my' wrens chose to go to bed. The jackdaws' raucous cries completely drowned the confidential murmurings of the little birds I was trying to record. The thermometer didn't work either. It was sensitive enough to do the job, but if the wrens roosted close round it, it simply recorded their body temperature. If I placed it an inch or so above where they squatted in the box, they didn't warm the air enough to get a significant reading.

Success with such experiments doesn't come easily, and it wouldn't be much fun if it did. So I am little wiser than I was. As the days lengthen, perhaps the jackdaws will be less obtrusive or roost at a different time so that I can eavesdrop on the wrens before they come. But whatever success I have – or lack of it – nothing can diminish the pleasure of knowing that so many Jenny wrens are finding shelter in the box I made last spring.

# 49. Snowscene

I have never been able to test the theory that everyone has one leg shorter than the other, though I can well imagine that such researching might have its rewards. It is certainly true that most people do find it almost impossible to walk in a straight line without some landmark as an aiming point. If you have any doubt about this, go to the centre of a large field on a pitch black night and try to reach the gate without stumbling round the hedgerow till you happen upon it by accident.

I was once lost in a dense fog on familiar ground in the deerpark within half a mile of where I live. I got so thoroughly bamfoozled that, when I did eventually reach the park fence, I hadn't the least idea whether to turn left or right. The country explanation for such ineptitiude is that one leg (presumably the 'master' leg) is longer than the other and tends to drive one round in circles.

Wild animals and birds are not so inadequate. The law of survival of

Silver birches in the snow

the fittest would soon weed out such weaklings, and I rediscover the truth of this every winter.

One of the easiest ways of taking a census of wildlife is to walk quietly round the day after a fairly heavy fall of snow. The footprints that remain not only show who passed that way. They provide circumstantial evidence of dramas no one saw for all with the know-how to decipher such clues as flurries in the snow where a predator caught its prey.

Judged by a human yardstick, animals might seem as likely to get lost in snow as men. We take it for granted that they see as well as we can. The fact is that the eyes of many animals are not equipped to focus sharply although they are often more sensitive to movement than human eyes. Their protective coloration and camouflage is based on this, so that if a hare 'claps' (or squats, motionless) on plough, she is quite invisible to a dog though we can see her plainly.

Hares are well aware of this ability to do a disappearing act simply by freezing motionless. When a dog spots a hare moving perhaps two or three hundred yards away, it will often streak off in pursuit. If the hare accepted the challenge and ran for its life, the dog might catch it. But when it sinks into immobility, the dog often passes within a yard without seeing it though it is obvious to human eyes.

So it is clear that animals don't find their way as we do by navigating from one sharply focused landmark to the next, and yet they don't get lost!

I once had a tame weasel which would give a demonstration of this every time I took him to a party. He made my jacket pocket his headquarters and popped down to the floor to explore a foot or so of strange territory. When he had memorised it, he would whizz up my trouser leg, round the inside of my shirt and back to 'his' pocket as though he were pursued by all the demons from hell. He would repeat this party trick again and again, each time extending the scope of his foray until he knew the strange room by heart and could dive into my pocket from any direction as a reflex escape routine.

Animals do the same thing in the wild, learning their territory as much by touch and smell as sight. They do it so consistently that they wear visible paths, or runs, in grass and undergrowth, and generation after generation follow the same line of country, possibly because their forebears found by experience that they were the easiest ways to take. The ways they use to sally forth and scramble home to safety are so habitual that keepers can catch them by putting an unbaited trap in their run.

But they can't see the runs they have learned when they are covered by snow and they can't focus on some salient landmark as we would. Yet, by some instinct denied to our sensitivity, they still know where they are.

When I go round the morning after snow has fallen, I find footprints leading from every gap in the hedges and between patches of dense cover in the wood. I track rabbits to find which holes they are using and, by working round in circles, I can establish which thickets the deer like best to lie in. I follow foxes, which put their hind feet in the track left as fore feet are lifted, so that the marks in the snow seem to have been left by a creature with two feet, not four. (Cats make a similar pattern.) Sometimes there is a space of eight or ten feet with no tracks at all, showing when the fox crouched before he sprang. If he was successful, there will be a patch of feathers or a blemish of blood on the snow, where some victim misplaced his faith in camouflage.

There are always deer tracks in our snow, and marks left by pheasants and hares and, less often, mice and voles. This is not because such small creatures are rare but because they wisely tunnel out of sight and danger.

Sometimes I see where badgers have played in the snow, leaving slides as if children had had a toboggan there. Country folk also think that badgers have one pair of legs shorter than the legs on the other side to help them run more easily along the steep sides of hills and valleys. They would find it pretty difficult to return with their shorter legs on the lower side of the hill, if that were true!

The completely new world that appears under a blanket of snow doesn't cause animals to lose their bearings as we might do. They use exactly the same gaps in the hedge, the same runs among the trees and the same tunnels through the undergrowth as they do in high summer. When I have once memorised the spots to examine from their tracks in the snow, I know where to look for signs of them in mud, months later.

They even continue to use their traditional tracks when the physical landscape has altered. Whole copses and spinneys and patches of cover were ripped out of the deerpark, where I got lost, when it was reclaimed for farmland. But I still see tracks of fox and hare and badger in snow and mud, in exactly the same spots they crossed before it became a sea of plough.

If I had their sixth sense (or both my legs were equal?) perhaps I could get around as well as they do.

# 50. Saving the deer with a difference

Some of England's rarest wild deer are found only in and around the Mortimer Forest, near Ludlow. They are a strange variety of fallow deer which have hair as long and shaggy as collie dogs instead of the sleek, dense coats of ordinary deer. Most of this coat is up to five inches long. The head from between the ears down to the eyes is covered with curly hair, thick enough to bury your fingers. Tufts on the side of the head sometimes give the illusion that the animal has sprouted a second pair of ears.

The discovery of these extraordinary animals in the Mortimer Forest was first recorded officially in the journal of the British Deer Society in 1966, though there had been local stories about deer with curious coats for forty years before that.

Colour variations are more common in fallow deer that in any wild animal I know. The deer in our wood vary from black to beautiful chestnut with white spots. Completely white deer are not uncommon in deer parks and Honey, my tame fallow doe, has a coat to match her name.

The long-haired fallow deer are far more important because, so far as is known, there are no more like them anywhere else in the world. When such a freak appears among wild animals, the abnormality often disappears within a generation. The gene which produced it is usually recessive so that it is bred out and the offspring reverts to normal if it finds a mate with normal dominant genes.

For some reason, this has not yet happened at Ludlow. The freak long-haired deer are holding their own instead of dying out as the text books say they should. Scientists are unable to pinpoint the reason. If they can solve the mystery, the knowledge may be of great use to geneticists who evolve specialist varieties of domestic stock.

The chance to do so might not have arisen before the last war. Until little more than twenty years ago, foresters regarded trees as their only business and anything which interfered with them, even indirectly, was destroyed. Forestry Commission policy has mercifully changed for the better since then. Deer are now treated as an amenity, to be enjoyed by the public, and as many deer are tolerated in most Commission woods as the natural food supply will sustain. The surplus is selectively culled by experts with rifles and the venison sold as a crop.

In big areas of woodland, like the Mortimer Forest, the Commission is not always the only landowner – but deer neither know nor respect the boundaries on a map! It is therefore vital for all the landowners in the district to agree the total it is necessary to destroy and to allocate that number between them. If someone takes too many, the herd may shrink to danger level. If too few are destroyed, the surplus may spill over to damage crops on farms.

The District Officer at Ludlow has told me that strong feeling about the importance of long-haired deer poses the danger of accurate estimates being influenced by subjective opinion. He wants hard facts to formulate his management plan, so he has invited members of the British Deer Society to do a census of the total number of deer in the forest.

I confess that I shall find the chore of driving fifty miles before dawn a small price to pay for the pleasure of watching his long-coated deer at peace in their natural surroundings. When we have assessed the total population, the Forestry Commission and its neighbours hope to agree how many should be cropped next season and how many each should take.

This has worked well in the past, but venison prices have rocketed. Some owners may want to take none at all but, with several thousand pounds at stake, someone might fall for the temptation of taking more than his share of the crop. It is even tempting for foresters to swell the income of their budget with venison it took no labour to produce.

This might not be disastrous with normal deer, whose numbers could be left to recover naturally if too many were killed in one season. But the deer at Ludlow are anything but normal and I believe very special steps are necessary to conserve them. Their control is not just a matter of turning surplus deer into venison and venison into banknotes.

So the Forestry Commission and local landowners invited the Nature Conservancy, Deer Society and other interested people to form a management committee to draw up a policy to conserve and look after these rarities. Enclosures have been made so that 'normal' and long-haired deer may be bred and studied under controlled conditions so that the importance of these genetic sports can be evaluated and steps taken to conserve them.

It is a rare example of friendly cooperation between landowners and bureaucrats and conservationists.

# 51. Zones for ramblers?

Those who have sweated at harvest and frozen to their tractor seats at ploughing share the almost sensual rewards of watching their young crops grow. Only those who have fretted over flood and drought, and worried night and day about pests and disease, can really appreciate the relief that the sight of the first young corn of the season brings. Imagine your reactions at seeing strange silhouettes on your skyline just as you were enjoying the results of such labours. Imagine seeing a gang of strangers trampling right through the middle of your tender, cherished crop of wheat.

I took off my metaphoric hat to the farmer who recently found himself

Glencoe, a rambler's paradise

in exactly those circumstances and still restrained himself to a dignified complaint. The terse rejoinder in exchange for his courtesy was that 'it' was a public footpath and that 'anyone' had the right to walk there. What was more, he should have reinstated the footpath after he had finished ploughing. To cap the point, he was told that he was being selfish and that the farmer over the hedge had been most helpful by taking the whole party over his cowsheds and introducing them to his cows.

The danger of transmitting disease from one farm to the next seems to have occurred to nobody.

Still biting back his anger, the farmer explained that his ancestors had lived there for generations and, being courteous men, they had been happy to allow their neighbours to cross their farm to work and market. The original path they used had run along hedgerows and headlands where crops were not damaged by their footsteps. Since those days, tractors had replaced horses so that the fields had grown in size to keep pace with mechanisation. The hedges had been grubbed out so that old paths now crossed the middle of fields.

Nobody grasped the significance when he added that his herd of cattle was accredited free from brucellosis. His visitors simply pointed out that the law of the land allowed them to use established footpaths and, whether he liked it or not, there was nothing he could do about it. They were perfectly correct. Mumbling about his farm becoming a knobbly-kneed monkey-run, the farmer left them in no doubt that, whether they were right or not, they certainly were not welcome.

I can see both sides of the case and I believe that many footpaths across land that is intensively farmed are obsolete and should be closed. Damage by trampling to corn is obvious, but usually grows out unless it occurs near to harvest. The same traffic over pasture leaves fewer scars but it can be catastrophic.

Instead of ruining a relatively small area of corn, walking on pasture can spread brucellosis or undulant fever which is not only dangerous to cattle, it is transmissible to man.

When I grew up, it was known as contagious abortion and was common on many small farms. A cow would 'cast' her calf and transfer the infection to the bull when he mated her again. He passed it on to

every other member of the herd, which would go barren and the farmer
bankrupt as his milk cheque dried up. Even the farm was often worth-
less because nobody wanted to start on tainted ground.

It took time to realise that the complaint could by caught by men
because the human form does not appear as abortion, but as undulant
fever or brucellosis. It is a most dangerous disease because it is both
difficult to diagnose and to cure. It can be caught by drinking infected
milk or by direct contact with an infected animal and the symptoms are
headache, loss of appetite and a high temperature far worse than a bad
dose of flu. It is called 'undulant' because the symptoms usually cease
after a few days, but recur again after a time in the same way that
victims get recurrent bouts of malaria.

The Ministry of Agriculture has started a scheme to stamp out the
disease before it escalates to town populations. But it is very expensive
to get an accredited brucellosis-free herd of cattle. Every beast on the
farm has to have three clear blood tests at four monthly intervals and
failures have to be slaughtered. When approval is eventually given,
every beast is blood tested annually and samples of milk are tested
monthly.

The danger of spread from neighbouring farms is so great that a
double fence has to be erected so that it is impossible so much as to rub
noses with a beast that is not accredited. In practice, the disease is
usually spread by contact with the ground and walking from one farm
to another is the easiest way to do so.

So it is understandable that farmers should blow their tops when
strangers wander onto their land, especially after trampling round
farmyards known to be infected. Insult is added to injury when walkers
arrive locally by car and insist on rampaging round not because they
enjoy the scenery or for exercise, but to flaunt their legal 'rights'.

A few years ago, when it was trendy to worship the golden calves of
Leisure and Recreation instead of Work, 'multi-use' spread into the
planners' jargon. Planners supposed that speedboaters and sailors and
fishermen and birdwatchers could enjoy themselves simultaneously.
Ramblers and hunters, shooting men and motor racers were expected
to romp hand-in-hand over the countryside. It didn't work because the
loudest voice or engine always won.

Planning officers have tried an interesting experiment. They have zoned pursuits, allocating some areas for one and some for another. They designated picnic spots with amenities to 'honey-pot' the crowds away from quiet spots and created motorless zones where the minority who hadn't forgotten how to use their legs could go.

It would need a change of law, of course, but perhaps walking could be zoned as well, to the mutual good of both walkers and farmers. Areas of wild beauty and rugged landscapes are rarely farmed intensively and that is where walkers really want to concentrate. Farmers with small unviable farms might like to augment their income by allowing people to pay to wander where they liked instead of restricting them to the narrow confines of footpaths.

It seems reasonable, in exchange, to keep intensively farmed land clear of the spread of infection and use it exclusively to grow vitally needed clean food instead of opening it up as public playground.

# 52. A cry of terror in the dusk

This year I heard the first fallow buck groaning in our wood on October 3 and the last on November 2. This is an exceptionally long time for the rut or mating season. They are silent for the rest of the season except for occasional staccato barks of warning when something alarms or puzzles them.

I happened to be out in the wood at dusk a couple of weeks ago making tape recordings of pheasants going to roost when I was treated to an orchestration of deer barking. I had settled down, hidden by the banks of a deep ditch, half an hour or so before the daylight faded. It is one of my favourite times of day, and I amused myself for quite a while watching two hares feeding on young white clover with which I sow the woodland rides.

An old poacher had taught me years ago how to call hares by sucking air between my lips to make the sort of high-pitched squeak that leverets or young hares make when hunted by a stoat. The hares stopped feeding and sat up to listen. I paused for a while before sucking out another impersonation of agony and terror. Hares are by no means as timorous as they are painted. The bigger of the two, probably an old doe, cocked her ears and lolloped purposefully towards me. She reminded me of a gaunt, old spinster chasing kids out of the orchard with her brolly.

Stoats find the hind feet of hares far more lethal than any old woman's chastisement, though. When a hare locates her target, she rushes towards it, spurred on by mother love. She passes over her victim at full speed – so fast that its instinctive reflex is to cringe to safety instead of using the split second for a counter-attack. As she passes over it, the hare kicks down at her foe. Doe hares can weigh eight pounds or more and their hind legs are powerful enough to propel them in leaps which would not disgrace an Olympic jumper. A sledgehammer blow from those hind legs can knock out far bigger opponents than stoats. If it were not for this aggressive protection, triggered into action by the cries of fear of their young, hares would suffer far more from predators.

It must have given the old hare in our ride a nasty shock when she discovered that there was no young leveret squeaking out in terror, and that I was not a stoat. I don't think she ever saw me because she came upwind and skidded to a halt when she caught my scent. Once again, she reminded me of the old spinster, frozen in horror by a naughty word. Then she was gone, skithering a shower of pebbles from her frightened feet.

I am never certain if animals of different species have any means of communication, though most scientists, I think, would deny it. Perhaps fear is an emotion capable of breaking the barrier of enlightenment – or perhaps what happened next was sheer coincidence.

The fact remains that the wild deer in the wood became uneasy at the precise time the hare fled in terror from my practical joke. The next sound I picked up on my tape recorder was the staccato bark of a large, black doe fallow deer. She is an old favourite of mine and has been about our wood for the last four years or so. She is as wild and shy as any other fallow deer when I meet her off our ground, but she seems to know the dogs and I will do her no harm in our wood. We often walk along a ride within twenty yards of her, and though she keeps a prudent eye on us, she shows no sign of alarm.

When the hare panicked, it was quite a different story. The deer was obviously puzzled so she let out a couple of sharp barks to warn the other deer that something seemed amiss. By this time, the light was fading and I could just see her silhouetted against a clearing. Though I kept perfectly still, I must have made an odd outline myself. Only my head and shoulders protruded over the bank of the ditch and my burly form was thickly swaddled in an anorak. My ears looked larger than Red Riding Hood's granny's because they were encased in an outside pair of earphones plugged into my tape recorder.

It was too much for the black doe, who repeated her double barks and melted into the cover of the trees. Feminine curiosity is a powerful driving force and it soon triumphed over her natural caution. Within about a minute her shadow reappeared at another point of the compass as she tried to solve the mystery of the strange shape in the ditch. I leaned gently forward to turn up the volume, but this slight movement alarmed her again.

As she barked her warning on my tape, she seemed to be so close that she sounded as if she was belching into my ear. This time I thought she really had got the message and had disappeared for good, but she still wouldn't admit that discretion was the better part of valour. When she did return, it was too dark to see her but she worked round downwind until she got my scent and, for the third time, she barked her disapproval.

Although it was doubtless triggered by instinct to warn the herd of danger, it was still stupid bravado. If I had wished her harm and been armed with a rifle instead of a tape recorder, I could have converted her to venison quite easily.

While this little drama had been playing itself out, my tape recorder had been collecting another album of potential suicide. My real reason for being in the wood was to compile background noises for a radio programme on pheasants. Instead of keeping their big beaks shut when they fly up to roost, cock pheasants make a terrible song and dance about it. They clatter their wings louder than cymbals and utter raucous cries as they rise to the branch they've selected.

Scientists would say that it is territorial behaviour designed to warn rivals off their pitch. The snag is that it tells poachers where they are as well, so that they can creep around on moonlight nights shooting them as they sleep.

So, by the time I had made my recordings, I knew precisely where the local birds were roosting. I chivvied those in vulnerable spots to safer trees and plotted the areas to festoon with fine copper trip wires attached to hidden alarm guns. There is nothing like a 12-bore alarm gun blasting off in the middle of the night, even loaded with blank cartridges, to make roosting pheasants alert and to persuade intruders that there are safer pitches to poach.

# 53. As common as muck

The chances are that ninety-nine people out of a hundred who saw the bird overleaf wouldn't give it a second glance. 'Only a common house sparrow,' they would say. And, because it was 'common' it would be beneath their notice. A dyed-in-the-wool birdwatcher, weighed down by a rucksack that made him look like a tortoise, would grow suddenly excited by the same bird. Clapping binoculars to his eyes with one hand, he'd fumble for his notebook with the other and put a triumphant tick on his check list in the space marked Tree Sparrow.

There is very little superficial difference between a tree sparrow and a house sparrow, so you have to be quite an expert to tell them apart. Trees sparrows are slightly smaller, but that is hard to detect if you can't see them side by side with house sparrows. And tree sparrows often nest in holes, but that isn't obvious at first sight either.

The easy thing to spot is that a cock house sparrow has a grey crown to his head. A cock tree sparrow has a beautiful chestnut crown, a black bib on each cheek and a white collar as flashy as a new curate's.

Birdwatchers get excited by tree sparrows because they are 'nice' – which is ornithological jargon for rare. I doubt if they really are as rare as they are made out to be, because I think it is the specialists who recognise them who are uncommon. The number of rare birds reported often happens to be in proportion to the number of birdwatchers in the area.

Snob classes of rarity leave me cold. Some of the most beautiful and interesting birds and animals (and people!) are also as common as muck. No nightingale in a romantic wood sings sweeter than a blackbird in a suburban garden, and the rarest falcon can perform no more spectacular aerobatics than a common swift.

Only yesterday I was looking idly through my study window when a starling caught my eye. I lost myself in admiration of the superb glossy sheen on his feathers. 'If he was rare,' I thought, 'instead of common, folk would go on expeditions to film him for the telly.' The result would extort as many oohs and aahs as there are gasps of wonder at close-ups of a hummingbird.

The tree sparrow with his white curate's collar

It wasn't just his beauty which caught my eye. He was within a couple of yards of where I sat so I could observe what he was feeding on. His bill was as long and sharp as a dagger as if Nature had designed it to poke conical holes in the ground. A moment's reflection made it plain that, if he did shove his beak into the turf, the hole it made would clamp it shut so that he wouldn't be able to pick anything out. I was near enough to put the theory to the test by watching his action minutely. Sure enough he opened his beak just before probing around. He wasn't just probing blindly, though I couldn't make out whether his sharp eye spotted movement first or whether his instinct or experience prompted him where to try.

Whichever it was, he had a high percentage of success. He was hunting for leather jackets just below the surface, and when he pulled the first one out, I got another surprise. I expected him to swallow it straightaway, but instead, he gripped it by one end and thrashed it around as kids play conkers. It wasn't a spiteful good hiding – only humans do that – so there was obviously some logical reason for the effort he expended. At first, I thought he was simply trying to kill it before he swallowed. After all, a bellyful of leatherjackets squirming around inside him would not be conducive to an after dinner nap.

I don't think that was the reason. I was reminded of a white rook I once reared by hand. I fed him on hard-boiled egg and raw minced meat, a little bread-and-milk – and a lot of live food. He loved meal-worms which are rather expensive from the pet shop, so I bred some in tins of bran in the airing cupboard. He loved them so much that he soon cleaned out the whole of my stock, so I tried 'gentles' that fishermen use as bait.

Gentles is a 'nice' term for the larvae of bluebottles; the common name for blowfly maggots – and you can't get commoner than that! I soon found that, although gentles were much cheaper than mealworms, they were very indigestible and passed through my rook intact. The reason turned out to be that they had very tough skins and I found that, if I punctured this skin, my rook had no trouble in digesting them at all.

Perhaps the starling was applying the same technique to his leatherjackets. Their very name implies that their skin is pretty tough – and presumably indigestible – so it seemed sensible to bang them around until the skin ruptured before eating them.

Reflecting that 'my' starling was not only beautiful but interesting, prompted memories of the attractions of other common things. What is more friendly or attractive than a tame robin? What makes more fascinating designs and patterns than a flock of blue tits, feeding by your window from a basket of nuts? These are common birds as likely to bring colour and movement to the smallest city garden as to the wildest wood.

Lots of animals are as beautiful as birds but less obvious. You will find that by standing perfectly still, you will see more that goes on in the countryside than if you dress up in big boots and an anorak and tramp around for miles.

I was leaning against a tree the other day when the leaves at my feet rustled and I caught sight of what appeared to be a tiny jewel dropped on the woodland floor. It was no precious stone, but a bank vole's eye. I hadn't seen him arrive but when he blinked it caught my attention. There he was, sitting up as glossy as a little squirrel, twirling a hawthorn berry between his front feet.

Keeping still like this, I often see long-tailed woodmice collecting acorns and making their winter larder in a hollow hazel or ash; and I see shrews with pointed noses, squeaking animosity at each other. All these things are common almost anywhere. You may not find them in the tidiest gardens, which are too prissy to protect them, but the jungle of grass behind the garden shed, the undug kitchen garden and neglected shrubbery all have their delights.

You may not enjoy them as often as you might because you don't make the time stand still. But if you did, you would discover that common things are quite as nice as rarities.

# 54. A man for all seasons

Friends who live in towns are sometimes horrified when they come to our house in winter. Snow and ice and holly berries strike them as romantic on Christmas cards, but winter mud holds out less attractions. The seas of mire in our gateways make them-teeter on tiptoe as fastidiously as Persian she-cats; their centrally-heated complexions wither in our bracing winds. They gush with sympathy that we have to put up with such privations and tell us condescendingly that 'it must be lovely here in the summer'. They cannot understand what we do when the fine weather fades or how we pass the time.

I love each season in its turn, winter as much as any. When the leaves are stripped, I can see so much beauty that was clothed before – the delicate tracery of tender twigs was camouflaged in summer. The robust skeletons of ancient trunks, with their network of branches, have been concealed until now.

The sun rises in autumn before we get up, and I appreciate the luxury of lying in bed to watch it illuminate the ancient stag-headed oak beyond the pool. By keeping my head perfectly still on the pillow, I can see the movement of the sun as it creeps up through the branches. The reward of this disciplined immobility is that I can literally see time pass before my eyes.

Now that the mornings have drawn in, it is the season of haze and frosts. When I go down to the pool to feed the wild duck, I can often hear them quacking long before they are visible through the gloom. I see the silhouettes of nearby trees with the pool misty and mysterious in the background.

The sun rises in a different position from autumn and summer. It still comes up in the east, of course, but as the year wears on, it creeps more and more towards the south before peeping over the horizon. Instead of first being visible behind the stag-headed oak, it is now almost in the centre of the woodland ride before I catch a glimpse of it.

Nothing is more delicate or beautiful than winter hoar frost as it picks out each individual blade of grass or twig. Nothing is purer than untrodden snow, stretching away to the horizon. Nowhere is quieter or more lonely than the centre of a wood in the stillness of dense, undrifting fog.

I know our wood so well that the smallest track or winding path is as familiar as the lines on the palms of my hand. Yet, in a fog, trees loom up that I had no idea were there. I trip over fallen branches I had never noticed and topple into ditches that seem to have gaped open overnight as booby traps. It could be frightening in a strange place because it would be so easy to get completely lost, but fog at home is rather fun. It is a challenge in navigation without the penalty of discomfort as the price of failure.

I love the sounds of winter, too. As I write, the wind is whipping through the tree tops with all the melancholic fury of a gale in a sailing ship's rigging.

Surprisingly, birds seem to sing better in winter than in high summer. By July, they were exhausted from the labours of nest-building and rearing their young. Their feathers were moulting and sore so that they could not have felt that there was much to sing about. Now their plumage is new and brilliant and they are fat from the harvest. They are oblivious to the discomforts of deep snow to come, for they live only for the present. Life must seem pretty good.

Cock pheasants and tawny owls echo at dusk, and small birds soliloquise about the delights of woodland shelter and easy food. The dogs and I spend hours watching and listening to birds, and when too much leisure emphasises winds, there are plenty of ways of getting warm. There are logs to be split and carried, and hay to be carted to the goats. The fowlpen has to be littered with fresh straw so that laying hens get fit by scratching for their grain instead of loafing about waiting for 'welfare' meals. Winter at home is anything but idle, and I never find it dull.

However monotonous it might be to go out in all weathers to feed someone else's stock or crack the ice on someone else's bird bath, the same chores become a joy at home. However boring it may be to watch the clock till one is free to leave someone else's employment, there is great satisfaction when time becomes one's servant instead of master.

It is a pleasure to grow weary from hard work. And exposure to wet or cold waiting to see deer, or foxes or badgers on the doorstep brings a reward out of all proportion to discomfort. After such exertions, hunger is a sauce that sharpens the appreciation of good food followed by the bliss of a log fire. Such pleasures may be simple, but I would not swap them for all the glamour and dazzle of the most sophisticated places.

# 55. Steel jaws on the 'safe' perch

Pole traps were among the foulest instruments of torture devised by uncivilised Man and they were made illegal as long ago as 1904. This may suggest that it is about time to drop the subject and to sweep it under a convenient carpet along with other eccentricities of our forefathers. But, although we may delude ourselves that our culture has become much more refined since then, the Royal Society for the Protection of Birds has found it necessary to mount a campaign to enforce the law banning the use of pole traps. The director of the Society told me that he has had several reports of their use.

Hawks and owls like to perch motionless where they can spot movements in the undergrowth which tell them that an unwary mouse or vole has left the shelter of its burrow and is just waiting to be pounced on for dinner.

Gamekeepers exploited this habit by setting up posts or poles at vantage points, usually on the edge of woodland or in clearings, which hawks and owls perched on as readily as tits alight on a hunk of fat hanging near a bird table. As soon as the perch was being used regularly, the keeper mounted a pole trap on it. This was a steel gin with toothed jaws like a miniature man-trap.

The next bird, whether predator or innocent blackbird, which alighted on the pole, sprung the trap and was caught by the legs. Its struggles tipped the trap off the pole and left the victim dangling in torture till the time the keeper called on his rounds and put it out of its misery. This method was so efficient that it was rare to find a single bird of prey on any 'well' keepered estate.

At the turn of the century pheasant shooting was at its zenith and a large part of the country was still owned by a few great estates, which had not yet been torn apart by death duties. Keepers were a law unto themselves and they honestly believed that every animal with carnivorous teeth, from a weasel to a stray dog, and every bird with a hooked bill, was the enemy of game, and better dead. They slaughtered hedgehogs and otters and barn owls and kestrels with the same determination as carrion crows and wandering cats. The larger the

Pole trap, one of the foulest instruments of torture

variety of trophies on their gibbets, the higher they were held in their employers' esteem.

The fact that in such unimaginative times even the pole trap was considered cruel enough to ban by law, is a measure of how barbarous it really was. That it should be necessary for the Royal Society for the Protection of Birds to mount a campaign to enforce the law in this so-called enlightened age is quite incomprehensible.

Although I wish the campaign well, I have not got much faith in legislation. Every large shoot has such secret undisturbed places, inaccessible to the public, that any keeper getting caught setting pole traps must be stupid as well as callous. I believe that such practices will only be stamped out when those concerned are convinced that it is reasonable and wise to stop.

There are more fishermen than footballers and demand for good fishing is so high that a disused gravel pit filled with water may be worth more than the land before the gravel was extracted. If you own a few hundred yards of salmon river bank, it is as good as winning the pools. And some who spend their hard-earned brass on such luxury are unlikely to look with much favour on herons or otters that feed on their fish, or kingfishers that eat the fry. Tycoons think little of paying £1000 a year to join a shooting syndicate that rears vast flocks of pheasants and employs a keeper to see that they die only by his boss's guns. They wouldn't be rich if they didn't equate investment with return but, by the same token, they wouldn't have got where they are if they were too thick to see both sides of an argument.

Emotional squeaks from those who would ban everything they don't agree with are unlikely to pierce their armour but much of the havoc they wreak is bred out of ignorance by lack of imagination. I find that some of these shooting men don't even know the difference between a hawk and an owl, but are at once sympathetic when they hear how both have been badly hit by poisonous pesticides. It rings a bell with them because pheasants and partridges have died by the same cause.

When they hear how many English hawks are taken illegally as fledglings from the nest for the sport of falconry, they bristle because it reminds them of poachers. They can understand complaints about factory farming because their expensive game birds have also suffered from the removal of nesting cover and natural food. They are convinced easily enough that there is room in the country for widely differing pastimes and most of them are prepared to give as well as take.

The exceptions still lay poison and use all sorts of callous methods to eliminate anything which competes with, or preys on, fish or game.

Pole traps are the most obvious of these devices and anyone who goes into the country can help to bring them to light, simply by examining any prominent pole or post which serves no apparent purpose. If there is a trap on top of it, leave it where it is. Tell the police where it is and tell them that you are passing on the information to the Royal Society for the Protection of Birds whose address is The Lodge, Sandy, Bedfordshire.

# 56. The other Haw–Haw

I believe the best speakers would have long tails and four legs – if only rats could talk. I do not mean to cast a slur on professional politicians or amateur debaters for I am lost in admiration for their gifts of golden words. Their split-second choice of an apt or telling phrase leaves me green with envy.

I have often marvelled at the way a rat in a tight corner will size up the only way of escape and put his plan into action while I would still be floundering. If he could translate thoughts into words as rapidly he would easily out-manoeuvre the slickest verbal trickster.

I base this judgment on practical experience. One day when we were

The common brown rat

ratting, we had surrounded a pile of brushwood and the dogs had caught several big rats as they bolted from the ferrets. Then I noticed a tiny creature still blind and no bigger than a mouse, clambering high into the slimmest twigs at the top of the pile. I reached out mechanically and popped him into my jacket pocket.

Then I saw another young rat trying to get across the farm track. It was full of potholes deep enough to drown him but he'd gone round the edges and made for a rathole on the other side. I cut him off and put him in my pocket with his brother, marvelling at such an effective instinct for self-preservation. Neither was old enough to have its eyes open so this must have been their first experience of the world outside their nest.

Yet one had discovered twigs too slender to support the weight of a pursuing ferret and the other had not blundered in blind panic into the deep water of a puddle. It had skirted it without losing the direction of the hole where I imagine previous rats had left a smell as inviting as the promised land.

It was not the milk of human kindness which prompted me to rescue a pocketful of rats. I have never heard even the most rabid protectionist preach against ratting though it seems no less cruel to me than hunting any other quarry. I filled my pocket for the very practical reason that I thought they would do for supper for the ferrets.

By the time I got home, it had dawned on me just how marvellous that sixth sense had been to lead such fragile and inexperienced creatures towards safety. So I reared one by hand and kept him as a pet so that I could study him more objectively.

I called him Haw–Haw and he grew up sleek and shining with health and utterly fearless with me. So fearless that he lived loose in the verandah and could be relied upon to dodge into an old bird cage he used as headquarters if a stranger called. Because he was so tame, I was able to try out an old wives' tale to test its validity.

I'd often heard that rats love hens' eggs and will carry them home clasped to their breasts in ecstasy; but like so many interesting theories it proved to be only half true.

Haw–Haw loved eggs all right and seemed to know by instinct what lay beneath the brittle shell the first time I showed him one. He was wildly excited, pressed his sensitive nose to it and danced round it to try to locate a weak spot where the appetising odour seeped through more freely. The obvious result was that the egg rolled away from him so that he looked exactly like a circus dog playing football.

He danced from side to side seeming to dribble as neatly as a football star until the attack ended abruptly when the egg smashed into the wall. The first time this happened, it was accidental but the shell cracked and the delicious fluid oozed out. A fitting reward for any rat born under a star lucky enough to allow him to ride in my pocket and survive. He gorged his fill but I deliberately left it several days before I let him see another egg.

There was no doubt that he remembered what it was. This time, his instinctive excitement was tempered by reason. He not only knew what it was, but he remembered what to do with it. Instead of dribbling it at random, he aimed it at the nearest wall and smacked home his advantage with the determination of a cup-winning goal scorer.

So perhaps the story of two rats working as a team is not so far fetched. Lots of country folk claim to have seen one rat on its side or back clasping an egg in all four paws while another tows it home by the tail. I never believed this because rats are quite as selfish as humans and I didn't think them capable of such teamwork. But you have only to shuffle the cards of cause and effect and motive to make it a nap-hand.

It is always worth doing this because experience tells me that the most unlikely folk-lore often has more in it than pompous theorists would have me believe. I don't doubt the truthfulness of the chaps who observed the rats but I think the explanation might be not that they were trying to help each other but the opposite.

I think the first rat was probably clasping the egg to his bosom to guard it selfishly for his sole possession. The other rat was simply trying to drag his mate off the egg so that he could get it. The key question is whether they were intelligent enough to profit from the experience. When they had been through this ritual a couple of times, could they harness cause and effect? Could they reason that this modicum of accidental cooperation had produced more eggs to be eaten more easily and in a safer place?

My guess is that they could.

# 57. Homes to rent

There is no need to be a skilled cabinet maker or a millionaire to have in your garden nest boxes that birds will find attractive. Last year, we put up ten boxes for tits and eight of them were occupied, three having two broods in the season.

An open-fronted box outside the kitchen window provided hospitality for a brood of spotted flycatchers, followed by a brood of wagtails after they fledged. Redstarts have nested in a box in the paddock three years out of four. The garage seems to be more popular still. Three swallow nests, and a pair of blackbirds reared two broods in a nest above my work bench. The wagtails that hatched first time by the kitchen window came onto the ledge above the garage door for their second family.

There are several reasons for this high density of nesting birds so close to the house. Of course, luck plays a great part. We live with one thousand acres of woodland on two sides and farmland on the other two. The pool across the paddock is surrounded with marsh, reeds, bracken and thicket which complete an unusual choice of nesting sites. So it is by good fortune that woodland birds and birds that prefer more open country converge here and explore our land thoroughly.

If you add a little management to whatever luck you have, you will improve the odds on birds that visit your neighbourhood settling down with you. I begin by keeping all sorts of food on the bird table and under low shelters along the edge of the wood all winter. I feed our four dogs mainly on raw meat, so there is plenty of fat which I cut off for my wife to melt in a saucepan. She pours this into basins and pushes old crusts, dog biscuits, crumbs and cattle nuts into the fat before it solidifies. When it is turned out, it is a neat basin-shaped fatty cake which I transfix with wire and hang by the window. A constant procession of blue tits and marsh tits, great tits and coal tits reward us by giving it no peace till they have scoffed the lot.

A local firm of corn millers lets me have the sweepings from their granary floor. This comes as a wonderful mixture of wheat and oats and barley and cattle cake and maize and ground meal of all sorts. It also

contains a fair proportion of cigarette packets and fag ends. But beggars
can't be choosers and I hope they will diminish when the campaign
against smoking begins to bite. I put this waste under the shelters along
the wood and it attracts mixed flocks of finches and pheasants and
woodpigeons and stock doves. Tunnel traps set nearby control the
numbers of rats and grey squirrels it would also attract, for tunnel traps
are patient guardians.

It so happens that we have an unusually high number of predators
because a huge flock of carrion crows uses our wood as a winter roost.
The only really effective way of getting rid of them would be to shoot the
wood so hard that almost everything else would be driven out in the
process. So I bump off what I can quietly and suffer the rest. A great
many of the birds that find food and comfort here in winter would like to
stay and breed. All that puts them off is the gang of enemies that share
the wood. Artificial nesting cover will eventually help as much as
feeding to attract them. So I have planted six hundred yards of mixed
hawthorn and blackthorn hedge along the edge of the drive as nesting
cover and to deter trespassers. And in woodland clearings, I put all the
rhododendrons and berried shrubs I can scrounge. This will give food
and shelter when I am growing whiskers, but for some years yet the
immediate surroundings of the house will be the safest place to rear a
family.

The proof of this is the number of birds that overcrowd the garage.
They put up with each other's nearness simply because it is a lesser evil
than the crows, jays, magpies and grey squirrels that are too numerous
outside. I cash in by putting nest boxes all around the house.

They are not the trendy olde worlde contraptions sold in shops, but
rough boxes. They are knocked together by my unskilled hands from
unplaned boards or hollow logs I find in the wood. The Royal Society
for the Protection of Birds, at The Lodge, Sandy, Bedfordshire, do an
excellent booklet with useful sketches and dimensions for boxes
designed to attract a wide variety of birds. I model mine more or less to
their designs.

Some of the dimensions are critical. For example, an entrance hole of
an inch-and-a-quarter diameter will let in tree sparrows and great tits
that may drive off smaller blue and coal tits. A hole a sixteenth smaller

will keep out the large birds, so it is often possible to pick and choose what feathered neighbours you want. Boxes put up now are likely to be used for roosting and the same birds will be more likely to nest there than if the box arrived only just in time for the nesting season.

I don't confine myself to conventional boxes. Last year I nailed strips of bark to oak trees to make narrow crevices. Tree creepers viewed them so often that they almost signed the contract. But it's no use counting your deposit till it's pouched, though I'm hoping for better luck this year.

An old willow blew down in the wood and we sliced it into sections with a wailing chain saw, choosing pieces where there were natural entrance holes. I have boarded the top and bottom of a couple of these sections and put them in trees where I hope the owls will find them attractive.

It is often possible to get more satisfaction from an intimate friendship with quite common birds than from a casual acquaintance with the most exotic rarities.

# 58. Winter woods

When it begins to snow, I am as delighted as a child with a new toboggan. Not that I have any ambitions to go winter-sporting because I fear my bulk would bury such a hazardous toy in the first snowdrift I encountered.

I am happy because the snow tells secrets which might otherwise remain hidden for the rest of the year. Animals and birds cannot avoid leaving evidence which betrays their secret hiding places and escape routes that I should never stumble on otherwise. It gives me the excuse to leave my typewriter and take the dogs out in the wood, not so much to see what there is about as to assess what has been there during the night before. It gives me the chance by unravelling the tracks, to calculate where creatures have come from and where they have gone.

Such virginal purity is deceptive. The superficial whiteness is not as

A roe deer searching for food through the snow

unsullied as it appears. Through the window of my study the woodland rides ribbon away to infinity without an apparent crease or blemish but when I go out and walk up them, it is obvious that I am by no means the first to ruffle their serenity.

Some time ago, I watched two foxes skimming in circles as graceful as skaters in a courtship dance. The vixen led him on and on and round and round till I feared his energy would flag before he caught her. Then their rhythm slowed, not because they tired but because the desire of the quarry was no longer to be chaste. Not wanting the wood infested with fox cubs at pheasant nesting time, I picked up my rifle and went out to stalk them.

I was not sorry that by the time I emerged, they had vanished into thin air, because it would have seemed churlish to have nipped such ardour in the bud. In any case, I had not had the pleasure of seeing a fox for some weeks, so that my finger was by no means itching for his execution. A few foxes do more good than harm by thinning out weaklings among other species besides putting a merciful end to wounded birds which have crept home to die after the shooters have been in the district.

I got quite a jolt when I went out after the last snow. Every ride I went along seemed to have been criss-crossed by regiments of foxes till I marvelled that they had not eaten every living thing as voraciously as a swarm of locusts. I chided myself for not being sharp enough to take the chance I had had with my rifle.

Not that picking off an odd one would appear to have made much difference among so many, so I wandered round the perimeter fence trying to decide whether the foxes in my wood had invaded over my boundary to plague the creatures to which I give sanctuary. The thought did cross my mind that it might be me who was harbouring cohorts of uninvited guests which were sallying forth at night to harass my neighbours.

By the time I had examined the whole length of the fence, which stretches over a couple of miles, I had come to the conclusion that I had blown up the whole affair out of proportion. The foxes were not residents but had come into our wood and now that I know their precise runs through the netting they are using, I shall ambush them if they persist.

When they had been in the wood, they had certainly gone over it with a nit-comb. It seemed to me to be thoroughness by a few rather than an expedition by a multitude which had left so many tracks, because they used only four runs through the netting, which would have been padded solid if many animals had used them. I know all the holes that foxes or badgers could use as earths and none of them had been used by a fox, so the responsibility of controlling them lies with my neighbour!

The snow had other tales to tell. I am out in the wood longer than most people would have the chance to be, and even when I am in the house I see deep into the trees from my study window. Although I reckon to know most of what goes on, at least in daylight, the snow showed browsing on patches of bilberry I hadn't even noticed. An old holly tree had been stripped to the height that deer can reach, as ancient trees in stately parks are trimmed neatly by the cattle.

I saw where a pheasant had been feeding. It had scratched a bare patch through the snow, apparently knowing by instinct where green clover leaves were hidden. When it had flown away, its wings had left their mark on the soft surface. The size of the wings was brilliantly etched into the white crystals, each individual flight feather curved under the stress of take-off as clearly as if frozen in flight by electronic flash photography.

It was very wet snow, which the weatherman said (quite wrongly!) would soon turn to rain but, instead of being swilled off, the build-up bent the branches till they creaked, sorting sound wood from the rotten, which cracked and fell.

By the next day, the woodland floor was as untidy as a sleazy barber's shop, littered with the unheeded clippings and combings of his trade. Tiny tracks, no bigger than match heads, betrayed the presence of wood mice and voles, and what appeared to be the grisly evidence of tragedy turned out to be no worse than the scarlet of yew berry skins discarded by a flock of feasting fieldfares.

There is no silence quite like the quiet of dense trees under a blanket of snow, and nowhere on earth more beautiful than an English wood in winter.

# Index